IMAGES
of Sport

CARDIFF RUGBY
FOOTBALL CLUB
1940-2000

Cardiff Rugby Squad in January 2001. From left to right, back row: Damien Geraghty, Phil Wheeler, Craig Quinnell, John Tait, Steve Moore, Emyr Lewis, Martyn Williams, Gary Powell. Middle row: Craig Morgan, Dan Baugh, Peter Rogers, Gareth Thomas, Wayne Fyvie, Gregori Kacala, Martin Morgan, Owain Williams, Mike Voyle, Nick Walne, Kenneth Fourie, Jamie Robinson, Lee Davies, Ian Jones, Pieter Muller. Front row: Rhys Williams, Ryan Powell, Spencer John, Andrew Lewis, Mike Rayer, Jonathan Humphreys, David Young (captain), Robert Howley, Neil Jenkins, Kevin Ellis, Paul Jones, Owain Ashman.

IMAGES
of Sport

CARDIFF RUGBY
FOOTBALL CLUB
1940-2000

Compiled by
Alan Evans and Duncan Gardiner

TEMPUS

First published 2001
Copyright © Alan Evans and Duncan Gardiner, 2001

Tempus Publishing Limited
The Mill, Brimscombe Port,
Stroud, Gloucestershire, GL5 2QG

ISBN 0 7524 2181 6

Typesetting and origination by
Tempus Publishing Limited
Printed in Great Britain by
Midway Clark Printing, Wiltshire

Also available from Tempus Publishing

Glamorgan CCC	Andrew Hignell	Images	0 7524 0792 9	£9.99
Glamorgan CCC 2	Andrew Hignell	Images	0 7524 1137 3	£9.99
Glamorgan CCC	Andrew Hignell	Classics	0 7524 1879 3	£12.00
Lord's: Cathedral of Cricket	Stephen Green	226pp hb	0 7524 2167 0	£25.00
Cardiff City FC, 1899-1947	Richard Shepherd	Images	0 7524 0666 3	£9.99
Cardiff City FC, 1947-1971	Richard Shepherd	Images	0 7524 0791 0	£9.99
Cardiff City FC, 1971-1993	Richard Shepherd	Images	0 7524 2068 2	£9.99
The Football Programme	John Litster	172pp sb	0 75241855 6	£12.99
Merthyr Tydfil FC	David Watkins	Images	0 7524 1813 0	£9.99
Newport County FC, 1912-1960	Richard Shepherd	Images	0 7524 1081 4	£9.99
Swansea Town FC, 1912-1964	Richard Shepherd	Images	0 7524 1133 0	£9.99
Voices of Vetch Field	Keith Haynes	Images	0 7524 1592 1	£9.99
Blackheath RFC	Dave Hammond	Images	0 7524 1688 X	£9.99
Bristol RFC	Mark Hoskins/Dave Fox	Images	0 7524 1875 0	£9.99
Cardiff RFC 1876-1939	Gardiner/Evans	Images	0 7524 1608 1	£9.99
The Five Nations Story (hardback)	David Hands	172pp hb	0 7524 1851 3	£18.99
Llanelli RFC	Bob Harragan	Images	0 7524 1134 9	£9.99
Newport RFC, 1874-1950	Steve Lewis	Images	0 7524 1570 0	£9.99
Newport RFC, 1950-2000	Steve Lewis	Images	0 7524 2084 4	£9.99

Contents

Foreword by David Young

It is impossible to play for Cardiff for any length of time without becoming aware of the rich history of the club. Its heritage is everywhere, not just in the photographs and trophies and mementoes that can be found in the clubhouse, but it almost seems to be in the air at Cardiff Arms Park.

I joined Cardiff as a twenty-one-year-old in 1988. I had already played for Wales but I knew that was not a guarantee of success with my new club. Everyone who comes to Cardiff has to prove himself on merit. Luckily, I did that and at the end of my first season I won selection for the British Lions, who were about to tour Australia. I felt very proud for myself and also for my club as I knew that I was following in the footsteps of great players like Gareth Edwards, Gerald Davies, Bleddyn Williams and about forty others who had been good enough to tour with the Lions.

The strength of the club, though, is not built on the so-called stars but on the great club men who year in, year out play their hearts out in the blue and black jersey. In my first period at the Arms Park the backbone of the team was provided by the likes of Howard Stone, Mike Rayer, Mark Edwards, Jeff Whitefoot and Tim Crothers. Some of them were internationals, others were not.

That first period at the club ended when I went to play rugby league at the end of 1989. I returned to the rugby union fold when the game went professional seven years later and, whatever the changes in how the club was run, I immediately realised that the traditions had stayed the same. A new generation of players had come along and there was a full-time staff running the club from day-to-day but the style and the ambition and the emphasis on standards had remained unchanged. Former players like John Nelson, Lloyd Williams, Colin Howe, Ian Robinson, Mervyn John and many others were still a huge influence on what made the club tick – and that's how it still is today.

We have entered a new century but the traditions live on. When I was fortunate enough to be chosen as captain for a third consecutive season in September 2000, the team manager was another great player and club man, Robert Norster. He had been captain in my first season at the club twelve years before. One of the coaching staff was Geraint John. He had been fly-half in that team in the 1980s. The chairman of the rugby committee was Robert Lakin whose blood, I swear, is blue and black and the chairman of the professional club was Peter Thomas, a hooker for Cardiff Athletic more than thirty-five years before.

Such a heritage will never be forgotten by the people who were part of it. It also needs books like this one to record the achievements of the present as well as remember the great days of the past. Alan Evans and Duncan Gardiner have done a great job in collecting the photographs in the pages that follow and a lot of us will get many happy hours from poring over them.

Introduction

When does history commence? The real beginning was, of course, covered in the companion volume to this book, *Images of Sport – Cardiff Rugby Football Club 1876-1939*, during which the club first forged a world-wide reputation for style, personalities and charisma. However, the sixty or so years which have followed the Second World War have also been filled with so many players whose names became familiar to the rugby world that selection becomes unenviable. It is, therefore, inevitable that some may feel that their heroes have not been mentioned enough while others have perhaps been afforded too much of the glory. Indeed, the problems that faced the club in 1999 over its initial Hall of Fame membership of fifteen illustrated fully the difficulties of narrowing such a talented field.

Just take two positions as an example – the half-backs. Immediately after the war it was Haydn Tanner and Billy Cleaver, rapidly followed by the redoubtable partnership of Rex Willis and Cliff Morgan. Later there came Gareth 'Prince' Edwards and Barry 'King' John, then Terry Holmes and Gareth Davies. Today, it is Rob Howley and Neil Jenkins while there are aficionados of the early 1990s who would argue the claims of Andy Moore and Adrian Davies.

Was there any pair of centres to match Jack Matthews and Bleddyn Williams? Any front row to equal Ian Eidman, Alan Phillips and Jeff Whitefoot, or a number eight the likes of John Scott, or a wing like Gerald Davies or a lock like Bob Norster? Where do record points-scorer Gareth Davies and giant lock Keith Rowlands or stalwarts like Mike Hall fit in? Where would you place club characters like Stan Bowes? Then again maybe this undeniably illustrious selection does not represent your favourites: it depends on your viewpoint. On top of all the heroes to be included there are the events off the field of play – for instance the changes to the ground since a German bomb dropped on the Arms Park in 1941.

The home and the persona of Cardiff RFC and the game in general has changed greatly in the past sixty years and perhaps nostalgia, as they say, ain't what it used to be. Yet, as the format of rugby football has moved inevitably with the times, interest in the past has arguably never been greater. Clubhouses still throb with the memories of yesteryear, debates about the qualities and comparison of players grow louder as the pints go down, complaints that things have changed only for the worse – 'the older I get the better I was' syndrome – continue apace. 'Twas ever thus.

Yes, rugby football has indeed changed. Certainly, it has altered almost beyond recognition from the colourful and Corinthian years covered in the earlier book, which does not mean, however, that it has become a monochrome version, lacking in character and characters, devoid of individuality and incident. Cardiff Rugby Football Club has been and remains among the foremost initiators of change and improvement, continuing to justify its position among the best-known club sides in the world. The number of overseas visitors to the Hubert Johnson Trophy Room in the clubhouse clearly testifies to the regard and curiosity about a famous institution, brought about by on-the-field dramas.

In the decades immediately after the Second World War, Cardiff teams took on and beat the mighty New Zealanders and Australians, just as they had earlier in the century. In one season no fewer than eleven Cardiff players were chosen to play for Wales. Nor was it only the elite who were proud to wear the blue and black. The club was, in 1949, one of the first to introduce a Youth XV and has since been one of only a few senior clubs in the country to maintain a continual record of youth teams up to the present day. Many leading players – some of whom have moved elsewhere – have started their careers at this level, an argument conveniently ignored by those who refer disparagingly to the capital city club as 'Chequebook Charlies'. Famous faces, famous teams, famous tries, famous matches; because of the plethora of potential personalities and incidents, somebody's favourite may well have slipped through the net, the role played by some individuals has not been fully illustrated. What does appear is nonetheless an evocative and dynamic visual journey through the rich history of one of the most fascinating clubs in the rugby world.

Acknowledgements

If we had thought that, in producing the earlier volume of a pictorial history of Cardiff Rugby Football Club (dealing with the years from its formation in 1876 to 1939 and the outbreak of the Second World War), we had overcome the really difficult task – caused largely by the paucity of photographic coverage – then we were naively misguiding ourselves.

The post-war years have produced so many famous matches, famous names, characters and ground transformations, quite apart from the inexorable move to cups, leagues and professionalism, that we faced the problems of selectors burdened with a glut of talented players. Even a squad system, in an era when multi-substitutions are permitted, could not accommodate the myriad magic moments that have carried Cardiff to its eminent position within the game.

The search for club memorabilia continues with the hope that a fully-fledged museum will be opened one day; the authors would be happy to hear from anyone who knows of historic items, of whatever kind, that might happily find a home in such a project.

Many people have contributed to this second volume and we particularly wish to thank Huw Evans, whose picture agency continues to produce sports photography of the highest quality, Colin Howe, a former prop forward and club official who has allowed us access to both the club's and his personal mementoes, and Ifor Davies of the Print Partnership who gave us valuable technical assistance.

Nor could this book have been produced without the help of Roger Beard, John Billot, Helena Braithwaite, Michael Casey Photography, Ann Davies, Simon Down, Vanessa Evans, Peter Goodfellow, Hansard, Richard Hudson, Maldwyn James, Mervyn John, Les Manfield, Jack Matthews, Haydn Morris, Barbara Nelson, Jim O'Donnell, David Owen, Alun Priday, Gwyn Rowlands, Mike Ryan, Derek Stears, the late Dennis Stephens, the Welsh Rugby Union, Bleddyn Williams, C.D. Williams, John Huw Williams and Lloyd Williams.

Alan Evans and Duncan Gardiner
Cardiff
2001

One
War and Peace

During a heavy bombing raid on the city on 2 January 1941, a landmine severely damaged the Cardiff Arms Park north stand under which Babs Filer, the stewardess, was clearing up the club bar. The match referred to in the cartoon by J.C. Walker (from the *South Wales Echo & Evening Express* of 15 January), showing the groundsman Jim Pursey with an American visitor, was between Wales and England in March 1940 for wartime charities. Happily, Babs (who had taken the job in 1930 and was to remain until the 1970s: see the companion volume dealing with the club from 1876-1939) was unhurt, but the ground would not be completely repaired until 1949, with the result that other wartime internationals had to be played elsewhere (although some club games were organised).

To place in context the damage in the cartoon on the previous page, we should perhaps go back briefly to the pre-war days. The skyline had changed dramatically in 1934 when the Welsh Rugby Union, major shareholders in the Cardiff Arms Park Company formed in 1922 to buy the land from the Bute Estate, built a new North stand. Story has it that the Marquess of Bute took such a dim view of its black corrugated-iron backing, which he could see down the road from his Cardiff Castle grounds, that he foreclosed on the strip of land on Westgate Street, where there were tennis courts, and allowed flats to be built there in 1936 to block the view. The social side of Cardiff Athletic Club and the cricket and rugby sections moved into the stand's mezzanine floor and a small new pavilion was built in the corner of the ground where the Athletic Club now lies. The last county match was played on the ground in 1976, both Glamorgan and the Cardiff Cricket Club moving to nearby Sophia Gardens, and, by the early 1980s, not only had the club rugby ground been built in the grounds along with a hotel, but a new national stadium was also complete by the Empire Pool.

Come the year 2000, come the new Millennium Stadium – and the National Stadium had changed direction from East-West to North-South. However, the Cardiff ground was still very much a part of what is still known throughout the rugby world as The Arms Park. Whether it will stay that way is debatable.

A War Emergency Committee, under the joint honorary secretaries of Cardiff Athletic Club, Norman Riches and Arthur Cornish, helped by, among others, Brice Jenkins, organised some matches for the rugby, cricket, bowls and tennis sections at the Arms Park. This rare picture of a Cardiff side in 1942/43 includes (holding the ball in the back row) Billy Cleaver, who was exempt from military service as a mining engineer. Sadly, if inevitably, Cardiff players were to lose their lives in the war: Pat Cox, Cecil Davies, Frank Gaccon, G.V. Heslop, Ken Jones, Trevor Ransome, Howard Roblin, Ken Street, V. Neil Taylor and Maurice Turnbull would never return.

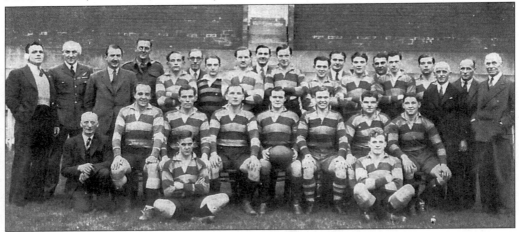

In May 1945, the Emergency Committee decided that the club should play once more on an 'official' basis, even though the Welsh Rugby Union had not yet resumed its peacetime functions. This group picture, taken early in the 1945/46 season, shows, from left to right, back row: Cliff Davies, Les Manfield, G.V. Wynne Jones (committee man and rugby commentator), Les Spence (recently returned from a harsh and prolonged spell as a prisoner of war with the Japanese who was to become president of the Welsh Rugby Union as well as Cardiff Athletic Club), G. Blackmore, Danny Davies, Cliff Morgan (but not the man who was to star for Wales and the British Lions), S. Davies, James Callaghan (MP for Cardiff South), H.E. Jones, B.V. Williams, Hubert Johnson (who was to become so influential as president of the Cardiff Athletic Club), D. St J. Rees, E. Morgan, G. Hale, Glyn Jones, Brice Jenkins, Arthur Cornish, G.E. Heslop. Middle row: J. Powell (kneeling), G. Tomkins, M. James, R. Bale, J. Matthews (captain), Bleddyn Williams, W.E. Tamplin, W.G. Jones. Front row: W. Darch, W.B. Cleaver. Many of these faces and their stories appear in the first volume of this pictorial history of Cardiff RFC; others will feature prominently in the following pages.

No sooner was rugby resumed after the war than Cardiff were off on their travels and spending the first peacetime New Year celebrations in France. On 31 December 1945, Cardiff beat Nantes 29-8 but, the following day, lost 19-18 to Union Sportive Cognacaise (Cognac) – the defeat partly explained perhaps by the fact that among their hosts were members of the Hennessey and Martell brandy families. *Above*: The teams line up for the Marseillaise in Cognac. *Below*: Billy Darch sets a Cardiff attack moving at Nantes.

Several matches were played for charities and on 1 May 1946 Cardiff Past met Cardiff Present to raise money for a Cardiff Rugby Club bed at the city's Royal Infirmary. The teams and officials were, from left to right, back row: G. Blackmore, T. Holley, W.E. Tamplin, R. Roberts, W.H. Jones, H.E. Jones, Ivor Williams, Dr Glyn Jones, G. Tomkins. Third row: L.M. Spence, D.E. Davies, Colin Jones, J. Cason, M. James, G. Lewis, D. Jones, St J. Rees, Duncan Brown, G. Hale, G. Porter, A. Turnbull, A. Coombes, Cliff Davies, B.H. Jenkins. Second row: J. Powell (trainer), R. Bale, H. Johnson, Dr J. Matthews, Sir William Reardon-Smith, W. Wooller (now back from his long spell as a Japanese POW), Bleddyn Williams, Ianto Jones, L. Manfield, R.A. Cornish. Front row: R. Knapp, J.E. Bowcott, W.B. Cleaver.

Mr James Callaghan, the Member of Parliament for Cardiff South in which the Arms Park stands and who was later to become Prime Minister of the United Kingdom, was responsible, on 17 April 1946, for a comment which has have great repercussions for the Cardiff club. During a House of Commons Budget debate on a concession in the entertainment tax, he referred, as can be seen from the extract in *Hansard*, the official record of proceedings in the House, to Cardiff as 'The city which has the finest rugby club in the four countries'. Predictably, there were protests from other members – led, it is alleged, by the MP for Llanelly (as it was then spelt), Mr James Griffiths – but the comment, regarded by some as arrogant, has also been exaggerated. Indeed, the club's official history, written by Danny Davies for the centenary year of 1976, overemphasised the statement by being titled *The Greatest*.

On Armistice Day, 11 November 1946, Cardiff were on their travels again – and this time broke new ground by flying for the first time. On Saturday 9 November, they beat Newport 11-0 at the Arms Park, and were to fly next day to Nantes, only to be delayed by bad weather in France. At 7 a.m. on the Sunday, however, a phone call reported improved weather and the party was asked to be at Pengam Airport, on the outskirts of Cardiff, for 1 p.m. to meet the plane (above, with the club group), which was a captured German Junkers Ju-52. To clear customs, it landed at Bristol, from which it was now too late to fly. Finally, the party left at 8 a.m. on Monday. Cardiff won 22-5 in front of a full house and for part of the return journey, during which the plane flew over the Arms Park, Bleddyn Williams, seen with Jack Matthews in service uniform, took the controls.

After the successful post-war season, Jack Matthews was elected captain for a second term in 1946/47, but he was called up for army service as a doctor and had to share his playing duties. Even in the Army he was successful and he is shown here receiving the Army Rugby Cup on behalf of the victorious Royal Army Medical Corps from Field-Marshal Bernard Montgomery.

During the 1947/48 season, eleven Cardiff players represented Wales in the Five Nations tournament or against Australia. They were, from left to right, back row: Les Williams, Cliff Davies, Gwyn Evans, Les Manfield, Frank Trott, Maldwyn James. Front row: Billy Cleaver, Haydn Tanner, Bleddyn Williams, Jack Matthews. Inset: Bill Tamplin. Manfield, who was capped twice by Wales in 1939 out of Mountain Ash and who made a further four international appearances while with Cardiff after the war, took over the club captaincy in 1946/47 when Jack Matthews was called up as an army doctor. Prop forward Cliff Davies, affectionately known as the Bard of Kenfig Hill, earned 16 caps and was a British Lion when they won in Australia and New Zealand in 1950. He made 190 appearances for Cardiff. Another colleague on that Lions tour was Billy Cleaver (see page 36). Policemen had regularly featured in the club's XV and Gwyn Evans, who was to appear more than 100 times and be capped 12 times for Wales, later became a Chief Superintendent, while Bill Tamplin was a sergeant in the Monmouthshire force. Capped 11 times by Wales, he captained the club, made 252 appearances and, on six occasions, kicked more than 100 points in a season. Haydn Tanner played 25 times for Wales (see page 23).

Les Williams goes over for a try after being fed by Jack Matthews in an unofficial international against France at the Stade Colombes in 1946. Les has a somewhat dubious claim to fame. Formerly with Llanelli, he had the astonishing strike rate of 47 tries in 51 matches for Cardiff between 1947 and 1949. He played his final match for the club on 8 January 1949 and, on 15 January, for Wales for whom, ironically, he scored two tries in a 9-3 win over England at the Arms Park. Secretly, however, he had signed professional terms for Hunslet two days previously.

C. Derek Williams, generally known simply as 'CD' (but to irrepressible prop Stan Bowes as 'Seedy'), has a remarkable association with Cardiff RFC. Playing as early as the wartime matches in 1942, he was ultimately to captain the club, make 248 appearances (despite leaving the city for business reasons on occasions), win 2 Welsh caps and then become, successively, committee man, chairman and trustee of Cardiff Athletic Club. A double blue at Oxford for rugby and boxing – only the need to study prevented him winning a cricket blue – he was the Berkshire county half-mile champion and, as can be seen here, a bearer of the Olympic flame during the 1948 Games in London.

The legendary and larger-than-life Stanley Bowes was one of the most remarkable characters ever involved with Cardiff. Joining the club in 1938/39, when he won his Rags cap, Stan went on to make 184 senior appearances and earn a Welsh final trial. By 1952/53, he was captaining The Rags for a third successive season and, the following year, was due to make it four. In the event, he played 36 first-team matches, including propping victoriously against the New Zealanders (see page 32). A stickler for clubhouse etiquette (never wear a hat, for example, or swear in front of a lady), he was even more colourful off the pitch, as anyone will testify who saw his after-match song-and-dance act or heard his comments about those who wore black-and-amber. Stan lived for Cardiff and he was to serve more than twenty-five years on the committee before his death. During these years he was a familiar figure wearing a tartan kilt to run the line at traditional matches with Watsonians every Christmas. Kilts were later to be worn by other Cardiff men (see pages 45 and 58).

In May 1949, the Welsh Rugby Union appealed to senior clubs to 'establish junior and youth teams to send missionary teams to smaller clubs'. The first Cardiff Youth team included Lloyd Williams (second right, seated), who was to go on to captain club and country. He was not, however, the first Wales Youth cap from the club: that was Bryn Mapstone (seated at the end of the front row). The captain, holding the ball, was Peter Owen. Owen, curiously, was belatedly traced and presented with his Youth tie in the year 2000. The picture does not include another lad who played in the first match against Cathays High School – the team went on to win 17 and draw 3 of its 21 matches – namely Joe Erskine, who was to gain international fame as British and European heavyweight boxing champion and who is pictured below receiving an award for his title from Jack Matthews.

Jack Matthews and Bleddyn Williams off on the move yet again. Matthews and Williams ... virtually inseparable in the memory for Cardiff, for Wales, for the British Lions and the Barbarians. Furthermore, as the year 2001 began, they are still together on their travels to watch Cardiff and Wales wherever and whenever possible. Dr Jack, a formidable and ferocious tackler – 'the ball may sometimes go past him,' recalls one contemporary, 'and possibly a player, but never the two together' – who was 17 times capped by Wales (this at a time when careers had been delayed or interrupted by the war), captained the club in 1945/46, 1946/47 and 1951/52, made 180 appearances in blue and black, scored 54 tries and, to his astonishment, one drop goal. Bleddyn, who was capped 22 times, scored 185 tries – a total which was not to be beaten for more than forty years (see page 108) – in 283 appearances for Cardiff and, as the Millennium year ended, was president of the Cardiff Athletic Club. His tries included a club record-breaking 41 in the 1947/48 season, during which Cardiff won 39 of 41 matches played. This figure was one higher than T.W. Pearson's 40 tries in 1892/93.

Boxing Day 1949 saw the opening by his one-time Cardiff colleague, Rhys Gabe, of the Gwyn Nicholls Gates, a memorial to the great centre who had worn the club and Welsh jerseys with such honour in the early part of the century. A fund, sanctioned by the Welsh Rugby Union and Cardiff Athletic Club, had been set up in April 1939 and, quickly, £733 was subscribed (the equivalent of around £30,000 today). The fund ceased until after the Second World War when donations, plus an exhibition match, took the total past £1,600. The graceful wrought-iron gates stood at the Westgate Street entrance to the Arms Park until the Millennium Stadium was built in 1999.

Haydn Tanner and Billy Cleaver had been the scintillating half-back partnership for Cardiff in the immediate post-war years but, near the end of the decade, a second exciting pairing came into being with Rex Willis (left) and Cliff Morgan. Rex, a colourful character who joined from Llandaff in 1947, was the scrum-half who went on to make 208 Cardiff appearances, win 21 caps for Wales and be a member of the victorious British Lions team in Australia and New Zealand in 1950. Cliff, from the Rhondda, played 202 times for his club after joining in 1949, was capped 29 times for Wales and went to South Africa with the Lions in 1958. By then, Cardiff were already back on the world stage.

Two

Back on the World Stage

Though official international matches were delayed for another year, the end of the Second World War in the summer of 1945 was followed that autumn by the immediate resumption of official club rugby. The many overseas sportsmen still on national service in Europe meant that it was not difficult to form top-class touring teams. Cardiff had already played the Royal Australian Air Force and the New Zealand Services – and won both matches – by the time the formidable New Zealand Kiwis arrived at the Arms Park on Boxing Day 1945. Cardiff lost their seventeen-match unbeaten record, but only by a solitary try to nil, against a side that were to finish their European tour with only two losses in thirty-three matches. More importantly, the club had quickly re-established the great tradition of magical matches against Southern Hemisphere sides that was to be such a feature of the next twenty years.

The Wallabies were unbeaten after four matches but were hampered by several injuries against a Cardiff team in the early stages of one of its greatest ever seasons. Led by Haydn Tanner and masterminded by Bleddyn Williams and Jack Matthews in the centre, Cardiff maintained a fast, open game and, despite the hard tackling, scored two tries by D.H. Jones and Cliff Davies to win by 11-3. From left to right, back row: W.G. Jones, Gwyn Evans, Les Manfield, W.E. Tamplin, Roy Roberts, Elvet Jones, Cliff Davies. Middle row: Stanley Bowes, D.H. Jones, Dr Jack Matthews, Haydn Tanner (captain), D.E. Davies (chairman), Bleddyn Williams, Billy Cleaver, Frank Trott. Front row: Maldwyn James, Les Williams.

The 1947 game was notable for the relentless tackling on both sides. Here, Wallabies full back Clem Windsor clears his line as D.H. Jones closes in. *The Daily Telegraph* reported that the defences were so good that the only way to make ground was through the kick ahead and, with Billy Cleaver at fly-half, Cardiff had the perfect man for the job.

The famous Tanner dive-pass in all its glory against the Wallabies. Haydn Tanner, one of Welsh rugby's all-time greats, was no stranger to heroic deeds against touring sides. As an eighteen-year-old schoolboy he had helped both Swansea and Wales beat the All Blacks in 1935 and, three years later, played for the Lions in South Africa. Now, he added the Wallabies' scalp and, at the end of their tour, was to star again as he led the Barbarians to victory in their first-ever game against a touring team at the Arms Park.

When Australia returned to the Arms Park three months later, nine Cardiff players were selected for Wales. It would have been ten if Tanner had been fit and Cleaver, for the only time in his 14 internationals, was switched to full back. Ewart Tamplin was honoured with the captaincy and celebrated by kicking two first-half penalty goals that secured victory. Most contemporary reports hailed Les Manfield as the best forward on the field. The Wales team pictured here was comprised of, from left to right, back row: Alan Bean (referee), John Gwilliam (Cambridge University), Les Manfield (Cardiff), Emlyn Davies (Aberavon), Gwyn Evans (Cardiff), Ossie Williams (Llanelli), Cliff Davies (Cardiff). Middle row: Maldwyn James (Cardiff), Les Williams (Cardiff), Bleddyn Williams (Cardiff), Ewart Tamplin (Cardiff, captain), Jack Matthews (Cardiff), Ken Jones (Newport), Billy Cleaver (Cardiff). Front row: Handel Greville (Llanelli), Glyn Davies (Pontypridd).

The Springbok head in the Cardiff Trophy Room, traditionally presented to the first team to beat the tourists, still bears testimony to the supreme effort made by the team in running the visitors so close. Cardiff captain Dr Jack Matthews claims that this was one of the most important games of his career and one the club could have won. Spectators began to queue in Westgate Street at 9.00 a.m. and the ground was full with 55,000 fans long before kick-off. Cardiff led 6-5 at half-time and 9-5 early in the second half, but were eventually overhauled by a Chum Ochse try in the dying moments.

The flying Chum Ochse scores the winning try five minutes from time as he outpaces full back Frank Trott to get to Hansie Brewis' diagonal kick, inches inside the touch-in-goal line.

Bleddyn Williams scored many great tries for the club and this was one of the best. Alun Thomas had come in off his wing to combine with Cliff Morgan and Jack Matthews, before Bleddyn went jinking past his great Springbok opposite number Ryk van Schoor for this famous score. This gave Cardiff a 6-5 lead after half an hour.

Ochse kicks clear as he is challenged by Cardiff wing Alun Thomas. There had been speculation beforehand that Thomas might play in the centre, but Matthews and Williams shone there and he again proved to be a useful utility back. Alun Thomas eventually won 13 caps as a centre, wing and fly-half and toured South Africa with the 1955 Lions – where he played five times as a full-back. In later years he became a successful official, returning to South Africa in 1964 as assistant manager of Wales and, ten years later, as manager of the triumphant Lions.

Saturday 12 November 1953 was one of the greatest days in Cardiff's history. This is the famous team that beat the All Blacks 8-3 and whose survivors still meet annually to celebrate the victory. From left to right, back row: Gareth Griffiths, John Llewellyn, Eddie Thomas, Malcolm Collins, John Nelson, J.D. Evans. Front row: C.D. Williams, Stanley Bowes, Rex Willis, Sid Judd, Bleddyn Williams (captain), Cliff Morgan, Alun Thomas, Gwyn Rowlands, Geoff Beckingham.

A photograph of celebration fit for a famous victory. It was entirely appropriate that one of the greatest players in the history of Cardiff and Welsh rugby, Bleddyn Williams, was captain on this day. His pre-match advice to his team – 'We have got to try things … if we fail, we fail, but we have got to be different' – paid off spectacularly with two tries in the opening quarter. No man deserved more than Williams to be carried shoulder high from the Arms Park at the end of this historic match.

The build-up to Cardiff's first try after only six minutes became etched in the memory of every true Blue and Black supporter. A break from a defensive scrum by Cliff Morgan and his chip ahead and regathering of the ball led to Alun Thomas sending right wing Gwyn Rowlands racing along the south touchline. His crosskick, in turn, was pounced upon under the shadow of the All Blacks' posts at the Westgate Street end for the famous try. The scorer was Sid Judd who, remarkably, repeated the feat when Wales beat New Zealand four weeks later. Sid Judd captained Cardiff the following season but, sadly, died of leukaemia in 1959 at the age of thirty.

Dr Gwyn Rowlands was another Cardiff and Wales hero in 1953. He was a goal-kicking wing, born and educated in Berkhamsted with dual qualification for Wales and England. After playing in two England trials in 1948 while a twenty-year-old medical student at London Hospital, he joined London Welsh and then Cardiff and won the first of his four Welsh caps in the historic win over New Zealand. In six seasons at the club Rowlands played in 99 games and scored 66 tries.

There was no shortage of publications and souvenirs to celebrate Cardiff's famous victory over the All Blacks. This contemporary newspaper cartoon captures the mood of the day and is a timely reminder that, whatever the importance of the game, there was always room for a bit of humour. Even in victory there were hints of another great struggle to come at the Arms Park the following month, when the same New Zealand side would play Wales. That would be a test for the fans as much as for the players. As the note in the bottom left hand corner says: 'Anyone who can't hold his breath for the last ten minutes should get rid of his international ticket!' The newspaper reports of the time were unashamedly lyrical. One of them noted: 'Cardiff's victory against the All Blacks on Saturday was like a symphony on a football field, a masterpiece of design, an anthem of courage...'

NEW ZEALAND RUGBY FOOTBALL TOUR 1953-1954

REPRESENTATIVES OF THE
FOUR HOME RUGBY UNIONS

T. H. HAMER & CO. LTD.

TELEPHONE: WHITEHALL 6527
TELEGRAMS: NUZEALINES, LESQUARE, LONDON

7 HAYMARKET
LONDON. S.W.1

PEEB/MAI.

24th. November, 1953.

Hubert Johnson Esq.,
Chairman,
Cardiff Rugby Football Club,
Cardiff Arms Park,
CARDIFF.

Dear Hubert,

May I, on behalf of the Four Home Rugby Unions,
thank you and the officials of the Cardiff Club for the grand
welcome and Game you gave to the All Blacks Team on Saturday
last. I think you will know by now that although our boys
were beaten, they thoroughly enjoyed the Game, and greatly
appreciated the manner in which the victory of the Cardiff
side was gained. I am sure that we shall not meet a side
playing a better brand of Rugby Football during the whole
Tour, and certainly not a side with as great a Team spirit.

I was so sorry that due to a misunderstanding at
Cardiff Station you could not say good-bye to the Team. I did,
in fact, see you as the train was leaving the station, and
understand from Eric Evans that you were waiting for the
Coaches at the entrance to the Station. It was unfortunate
that both at the arrival and departure of the Team you were
not able to greet them as you would have wished, and as I said
before I am very sorry for my omissions on the first occasion.

Telegrams and letters of congratulation poured in from all around the rugby world. Typical of the spirit in which the game was played was one from Mr Philip Bradforth, the liaison officer for the Four Home Unions. He also worked for the tour's travel agents, T.H. Hamer and Co., although judging by the middle paragraph of the letter this was no guarantee of trouble-free train travel – even in 1953!

Another priceless memento. Post-match dinners have been a feature of touring team matches until comparatively recently and this particular one turned out to be the first of many to commemorate one match. Every autumn since 1953 the survivors of the Cardiff XV have gathered to remember their great achievement, often in the company of New Zealanders. Sadly as the years have gone by their numbers have declined – by the summer of 2000 only seven were still alive – but every year they unfailingly raise a glass to absent friends. The 2001 dinner was held in Cardiff on the eve of the Wales against England game at the Millennium Stadium.

CARDIFF RUGBY FOOTBALL CLUB

DINNER

In honour of the visit of the
New Zealand Rugby Football Team

21st NOVEMBER, 1953
ROYAL HOTEL, CARDIFF

Four weeks after Cardiff beat New Zealand, Wales repeated the feat at the Arms Park. Bleddyn Williams was again captain, ensuring him a special place in Welsh sporting history. With him in the national XV were five of his club colleagues, including Morgan and Willis at half-back and Judd, who again scored a try. From left to right, back row: Dr P.F. Cooper (RFU referee), R.C.C. Thomas (Swansea), Sid Judd (Cardiff), Rees Stephens (Neath), Roy John (Neath), John Gwilliam (Gloucester), Courtney Meredith (Neath), Ivor Jones (touch judge). Middle row: W.O.G. Williams (Swansea), Gareth Griffiths (Cardiff), Bleddyn Williams (Cardiff, captain), Ken Jones (Newport), D.M. Davies (Somerset Police). Front row: Gwyn Rowlands (Cardiff), Rex Willis (Cardiff), Cliff Morgan (Cardiff), Gerwyn Williams (London Welsh).

Gareth Griffiths was one of the five Cardiff players to share the unique distinction of being part of two wins over the All Blacks in the space of a month. At the end of that tour he lined up with Morgan, Willis and Judd as the club's representatives in the Barbarians team that brought down the curtain on the All Blacks' visit, again at Cardiff Arms Park. Two years later he was flown out as a replacement back for the Lions in South Africa. Here, having being called away from his teaching duties in Penygraig, he arrives in Johannesburg to join the tour in July 1955.

Another part of Cardiff's touring team folklore is that the club has never lost to Australia. Following the victories over the earlier tourists of 1908 and 1947, the 'Third Wallabies' were also put to the sword. A new club team had developed after the heroics of the early 1950s. The five survivors from 1953 were C.D. Williams, Morgan, Willis, Eddie Thomas and J.D. Evans. With them, by 1957, were future British Lions such as Kingsley Jones and Roddy Evans, the ultra-dependable full-back Alun Priday and the dynamic flanker Dai Hayward. The team's captain was Eddie Thomas, a no-nonsense number eight from the Rhondda.

Eddie Thomas (right) chases a loose ball against the Wallabies. He was captain of the club in his final season of 1957/58 and led the team to the unofficial club championship. The match against Australia also completed a notable personal hat-trick for Thomas: he had played for the combined Neath and Aberavon XV against the Springboks in 1951, for Cardiff against the All Blacks in 1953, and now for the club again when the Wallabies were beaten. He retired at the end of the same season with 217 first team games under his belt and the club's annual report noting that 'he worked as efficiently for the good of the club off the field as on it'.

Post-match celebrations are never half-hearted and victory over the Wallabies was the signal for a hearty song or two with the actor and erstwhile flank forward Richard Burton. According to legend, Burton said that he would rather play once for Wales at Cardiff Arms Park than play Hamlet. Joining him in Cardiff Athletic Club in 1957 are, among others, Sid Judd, Bleddyn Williams, Colin Howe and Cliff Jones.

One of the great traditions of the club is the annual reunion of the 1953 team that beat the All Blacks. The visit of the 1972 All Blacks coincided with the 19th Reunion Dinner at the Banqueting Hall of Cardiff Castle and another distinguished Welsh actor, Stanley Baker, toasts the club chairman that year, Hubert Johnson, and the All Blacks' coach, Bob Duff.

Three
More Golden Years and Players

Away from the matches with touring teams, the 1950s had begun with a game that was to go down in the annals of rugby worldwide. A record club-match crowd of 48,500 packed Cardiff Arms Park for the visit of Newport on 17 February 1951. The Usksiders were on the third leg of the elusive four wins in a season over their great rivals. They won this match 8-3 but two weeks later at Rodney Parade were foiled again when the two sides drew 3-3.

In 1951/52 Cardiff Rugby Football Club celebrated its seventy-fifth anniversary season in the best manner possible when the Lions tour party of the previous year reassembled to play a special match against the club. Another big crowd, of 45,000, turned up in perfect conditions to see one of the best exhibitions of open rugby ever staged at the Arms Park. Four of Cardiff's five Lions – Bleddyn Williams, Jack Matthews, Rex Willis and Cliff Davies – turned out for the club while the fifth, Billy Cleaver, partnered Jack Kyle at half back for the Lions. Cardiff scored four unconverted tries but lost narrowly 12-14.

A splendid forty-page souvenir programme, priced at one shilling, was produced for the match and this autographed team page gives some indication of the importance of the occasion. The two captains were Karl Mullen, the Ireland hooker, and Dr Jack Matthews.

Right wing Derek Murphy scores the first of his two tries in the opening ten minutes of the match, eluding Lions' full back Lewis Jones. In the second half Bleddyn Williams and Sid Judd added further tries but the draw that would have been a fitting result on such a day was out of reach after the final conversion from in front of the posts was missed. Murphy went on to score 77 tries in 162 games during his eight seasons at the club..

In front of the packed terraces the twenty-one-year-old Cliff Morgan gets away from the England and Lions wing forward, Vic Roberts. Morgan had already won his first caps for Wales the previous spring – the second one coming against France in Paris on his twenty-first birthday. Four years after this celebration match he was to become a famous British Lion himself when they toured South Africa.

Billy Cleaver makes a break in front of another large crowd in a local derby at Rodney Parade. He was one of the most effective utility backs of the early post-war years, good enough to play for Wales at full-back against Australia, in the centre alongside both Jack Matthews and Bleddyn Williams, and as fly-half partner to Haydn Tanner in three internationals and to Rex Willis in the Triple Crown and Grand Slam winning team of 1950. Later that year he toured New Zealand and Australia with the Lions, playing at full-back in the first three tests against the All Blacks to add to his 14 caps for Wales. Cleaver made his club debut against Cardiff & District in the first match after the Second World War and won his club cap with 33 games in that first season. By the time he retired in 1951 he had made 141 first-team appearances.

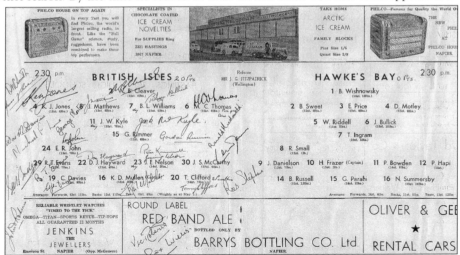

Cleaver played in 15 matches for the Lions in New Zealand and Australia and, as this rare autographed programme for the match against Hawke's Bay shows, they were indeed a star unit. Cardiff's Jack Matthews, Bleddyn Williams, Cliff Davies and Cleaver all played in this particular match with a fifth blue and black, Rex Willis, enjoying his afternoon off.

Cardiff's happy links with the rugby men of Nantes and Cognac continued well into the 1950s. In September 1952, on the eve of the first team's match with Nantes & Cognac, there was a veterans match for what was light-heartedly billed 'The championship of the world'. Cardiff won 20-3. The Cardiff players in the photograph are, from left to right, back row: Edgar Welch, 'Doc' Drummond, Les Manfield, Les Spence, Tom Holley. Middle row: Harry Rees, Wilfred Wooller, Maldwyn James, Lyn Williams. Front row: Gwynne Porter, Haydn Wilkins, Gwyn Davies, W.E.N. Davies, Billy Cleaver, Gwyn Evans. The oldest members of the Cardiff team were Les Spence, Doc Drummond and Harry Rees; all of them were aged forty-four at the time of the game and all played in the pack. The helpful match programme actually lists the ages of all the participants in the team line-ups, and from this we learn that in the French side there were two fifty-somethings. Paul Gringoire (fifty-seven) was the captain, and also a general bakery manager and the vice-president of the Nantes Chamber of Commerce. With him was his younger brother, Maurice, a mere fifty-four-year-old and listed as an assistant bakery manager. It was obviously a family business. In the programme's 'Welcome' page, particular mention is made of Marcel Pedron, a legend in Nantes and an honorary life member of Cardiff, who was unable to attend because of 'an important conference in Cannes'. It was club rugby of another age.

The Welsh seven-a-side tournament, later known as the Snelling Sevens, had started at Newport in 1954 but Cardiff, due to a congestion of fixtures, did not enter until the following year. Emulating their predecessors in 1939, who had won the Middlesex Sevens in Twickenham at the first attempt, the team, captained by Gareth Griffiths, beat Pontypridd, Aberavon and Newbridge, en route to a victory in the final over holders Newport. One of Cardiff's stars was Gordon Wells, who scored six tries in the tournament. The Cardiff team pictured here is, from left to right, back row: J.C. Crothers, J.H. Thomas. Front row: Ken Richards, Lloyd Williams, Gareth Griffiths, Gordon Wells, Terry Donovan.

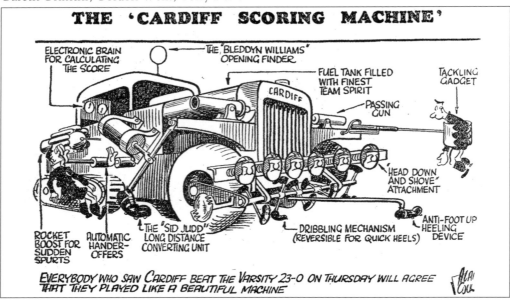

In November 1954 Cardiff beat Oxford University 23-0, scoring five tries in the process. The local newspaper, *The Oxford Mail*, neatly portrayed the merits of the Cardiff team in this cartoon – the vehicle even has a 'Bleddyn Williams Opening Finder'!

Bleddyn Williams, the Prince of Centres, retired at the end of the 1954/55 season. His final game was against Llanelli in front of 15,000 fans at the Arms Park on 7 May 1955. Cardiff won 9-3 and at the end of the match he was taken shoulder-high from the pitch by his team mates. The match programme had paid tribute to him in the best possible terms: 'His approach to the game has been ideal and he has never forgotten, despite his individual brilliance, that rugby football is essentially a team game … The open game with crisp passing and deceptive running is Bleddyn's idea of the game at its best … May he receive the acclamation of all for he has added lustre to a great game and brought added glory to a great club and a great country. He will be missed.' Bleddyn Williams was club captain in 1949/50 and 1953/54 and finished with 185 tries in 283 games for Cardiff. He won 22 caps for Wales and played in 5 tests for the British Lions. In 2000 he became president of Cardiff Athletic Club..

END OF GREAT BLEDDYN ERA

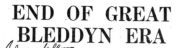

By WILFRED WOOLLER

NOW that the history of the 1954-55 Rugby season has been filed all that remains is to draw on those moments while linger in the memory.

First let me pay tribute to referee Harold Phillips, who controlled the final of the Welsh Sevens last Saturday to mark the end of an illustrious career of service to Rugby.

Many times have I played under the genial whistle of Harold Phillips.

He controlled international matches and club matches with a mild impartiality which made his 31 years in the game a pleasure to himself and to the many thousands of Rugby players who came under his jurisdiction.

He may yet have his greatest work for Rugby ahead of him for he would like to see a properly organised federation of Welsh referees, instead of the present slipshod method of W.R.U. control.

Ideal centre

Passing from the scene also is the most colourful centre of post-war Rugby, Bleddyn Williams. It is with sorrow that one realises that no more will a school-master be able to take his young charges to Cardiff Arms Park and say, with every confidence in the world, " That is how a centre should play the game ! "

Bleddyn was a craftsman the like of which we shall wait a long time to see again. There were periods in his career when additional weight reduced his speed and he lost his international place. There were games when latterly he was slow for his club but so masterly was his control of the basic arts of three-play that he could always pull something out of the hat. I wonder how many tries that superbly correct pass has made for his fellow players ? His dominion opponents had no doubts, for I am certain that Bleddyn Williams will

be ranked by them as the best centre produced in Great Britain since the war.

Paris, in the spring, brought out the international memory. Rees Stephens captained and led a Welsh XV to a magnificent victory at Stade Colombe. For the first time in the series the full power of the Welsh side was brought out.

A great win

This year's French side was a great one. They were very fit. They were playing on home soil. Rees Stephens was undismayed, and he took the Welsh team on to the field to win.

The tackling was at all times and by every player magnificent. It was no uncommon sight to see a French-man running one way with the ball one moment, and then to see him bouncing back the other the next.

From two such tackles came two Alun Thomas opportunist breaks and two tries for Wales. This was a great win by any standards and it proved my oft-stated contention that Wales were the strongest side of the lot.

Finally, a tribute to Cardiff in winning the Welsh Sevens at the first time of asking. As I wrote last Saturday, the sevens game demands strict attention to tactics.

That attention to detail has been a strong point in the Cardiff club since the war. It is a pity that the Cardiff captain on the day, Gareth Griffiths, is not (so far) going to South Africa. He is a better player than several selected.

Welsh Rugby .. By David Owen

Club, country will miss Bleddyn

THE retirement of Bleddyn Williams, prince of modern centres, from the game next Saturday, brings to an end a colourful career. Indeed, it marks the end of an era. There only remains Ken Jones of the great Welsh backs of the immediate post-war years, and at the moment I understand he will have just one more season in the game.

Jones is keen to equal, if not pass, George Stephenson's second-of-45 appearances in International Rugger. He has 38 caps to his credit, and next season's four internationals would do the trick.

Bleddyn Williams will be missed. A classical, easy player, full of quality and the true spirit of the game, he has been the best centre of the post-war years.

It is argued that he was better for Cardiff than for Wales. He certainly was a team player, and the smooth working of club football was probably better suited to his style.

He liked open football, and although he often employed close tactics when captain of Wales, he did not enjoy them.

In all, he made 22 international appearances; five times as a victorious captain, and was in the 1952 " Triple Crown " side. He has gained all the honours the game can offer, and all will pay tribute to his greatness.

Matthews' future

His great partner and friend for Cardiff and Wales, Dr. Jack Matthews, is retiring from the Cardiff club administration. I hear he is to join the list of ex-player writers on the game next winter.

In any case, he will resign from the chairmanship of the club, and is not seeking re-election to the committee at this month's A.G.M.

Dr. Jack, like Bleddyn, has been a great servant to the Cardiff club, and a great player. The club will experi-

ence difficulty in replacing these stalwarts.

Neath's local hero, and Welsh captain, Rees Stephens, busy hotel and cafe owner, and local J.P., is not to retire.

Bleddyn Williams will be remarkably fit, and quite capable of playing good club football next season.

Rex Willis, who declined an invitation to go to South Africa with the British team, is also going to have another season. Then he will hang up his boots!

It is always hard for players to give up the game, but as one former International said: "You're as old as you feel. The trouble is the bruises take longer to mend as you get older!"

Some newspaper cuttings and the programme cover from the final match.

Though Bleddyn had retired, the Williams dynasty at the club lived on. In all, eight of the brothers were to play in blue and black colours. Gwyn and Brinley had preceded Bleddyn but after him came Lloyd, who was also to captain club and country, Vaughan, Cenydd, Elwyn (who played for Wales Under-23 against Canada in 1962) and Tony. Between them they gave the club remarkable service on and off the field and three of them – Lloyd, Elwyn and Tony – each played over 300 games. From left to right: Gwyn, Cenydd, Lloyd, Brinley, Tony, Vaughan, Bleddyn, Elwyn.

Malcolm Collins feeds back from a lineout in another tense struggle with Newport. Alongside Collins in the white scrum cap is W.R. 'Roddie' Evans, a student at Cambridge University who was to go on to win 13 caps for Wales and play in 4 tests for the 1959 British Lions in Australia and New Zealand. Rex Willis is the player waiting to receive the ball.

Colin Howe, Geoff Beckingham and John Evans epitomised all that was best about Cardiff's forward play and general team spirit in the 1950s. Howe joined the club from Pontypool in 1952 and went on to play 263 games for the first team, plus 70 for The Rags, before his retirement in 1964. He also played in a Welsh international trial match and captained The Rags in his final two seasons, later becoming part of the proud tradition of former players who gave unstinting committee service to the club. He played against Australia in 1957 and South Africa in 1960 and managed the 1972 tour to Rhodesia. Beckingham was a great hooker whose playing career unfortunately coincided with that of Newport's world-class practitioner, Bryn Meredith. Nevertheless, Beckingham was in the Cardiff team that beat the All Blacks in 1953 as well as the Wallabies four years later and won 2 caps for Wales. He was another of the '300 club' with 331 first-team appearances. Like Beckingham, J.D. Evans won 2 caps for Wales, the second of them alongside his club mate against France in 1958. His own club tally was 338 games in ten seasons. A native of Mountain Ash, Evans died in 1989 at the age of sixty-two.

The Romanian national team came to the Arms Park in September 1955 and attracted a large crowd for a game which was won narrowly by Cardiff 6-3. This was no mean achievement as the same team, based around the Bucharest club side, beat Swansea 19-3 and drew with Harlequins. This unusual action shot, as well as giving an excellent impression of the ground, is a reminder that in the 1950s the players were numbered in reverse order to that used today: the full back was number one, the front row were numbers eight, nine (hooker) and ten, and the back row thirteen, fourteen and fifteen.

Peter GOODFELLOW Roddy EVANS Geoff. BECKINGHAM Howard NICHOLLS Glyn WILLIAMS Alan PRIDAY Lynn DAVIES

Brian MARK Malcolm COLLINS Colin NEWITT

Reprezentativa de RUGBY a orașului Cardiff

Malcolm GOUGH Peter NYHAN Kingsley JONES

Colin HOWE Glyn JOHN Terry DONOVAN Eddie LEWIS Ken RICHARDS John EVANS Eddie THOMAS

At the end of the following season Cardiff paid a reciprocal visit to Bucharest, playing two matches against Romania 'B' and Bucharest & District. This was a notable landmark again in terms of attendance figures: the match at Stadionul 23 August on 1 June 1957 was played in front of 80,000 people because the rugby match was a warm-up to a football international between Romania and the USSR at 'B' level.

The line-out forms in front of the watching 80,000. The seven Cardiff forwards, from left to right, are: Geoff Beckingham, Colin Howe, J.D. Evans, Malcolm Collins, Roddie Evans, John Nelson and Eddie Thomas.

Moments later, Malcolm Collins competes for the ball with his Romanian opposite number. Collins was one of the Cardiff club's greatest servants. He made his first-team debut against Oxford University on 29 October 1949, won his club cap at the end of that season and in the seasons that followed regularly played 40 or more first-team games. In the season of his club captaincy, 1955/56, he played in an incredible 50 of the 52 official games on the fixture list and retired at the end of the 1957/58 campaign with 306 games to his credit. He played against the Springboks and the All Blacks and also for the Barbarians and in five international trial matches without winning the Wales cap he richly deserved. In later years he was a respected committee man and club chairman but died suddenly in December 1985.

One of the great club traditions was the end-of-season tour to Cornwall. Between 1930 and 1974 they continued almost uninterrupted, except during the war, and were a hugely popular sign that a new spring had arrived. Off-the-field enjoyment was (almost) as important as results on the field. In the front of this Sunday morning group at the Old Success Inn at Sennen Cove are, from left to right: Bleddyn Williams, J.D. Evans, Colin Howe, Lloyd Williams and Glyn Morgan. Behind them on the left is John Dodd, a prop forward who went on to lead Neath for three seasons, and in the middle is John Crothers.

Typical of the spirit engendered by the games in the south-west of England is this rare line-up at Bridgewater with a Cardiff Invitation XV taken there by Bleddyn Williams and captained by Dr Jack Matthews. Joining Dr Jack and Stanley Bowes in Cardiff's colours in the middle row is another 1950 Lion, the hooker D.M. 'Dai' Davies. He served in the Somerset Police and was only too glad to 'guest' for his visiting countrymen.

Cardiff's tours went north as well as south. For the New Year of 1951 the club had played Northumberland and then Watsonians and repeated the adventure six years later. The opponents this time were Glasgow High School FP on New Year's Eve and then Watsonians the following day. Here, Peter Goodfellow (left) and Alun Priday are entering into the spirit of the occasion as they walk down Princes Street, Edinburgh, on the morning of 1 January 1957. Having surprisingly lost in Glasgow, the team exacted revenge on Watsonians with a 12-8 win. Goodfellow – never was a man more aptly named – played 240 games for the first team in eleven seasons and captained The Rags for four seasons as well as the first team in 1956/57. Equally adept in the second and back rows, he played in a Welsh international trial in 1956 when he was honoured with the captaincy of the Whites XV. Peter Goodfellow had been a captain in the Ghurkhas and could speak Urdu, but when in Scotland did as the Scots did: 'While I retained my dignity with a Cardiff blazer and socks, I wore the kilt in the traditional manner.'

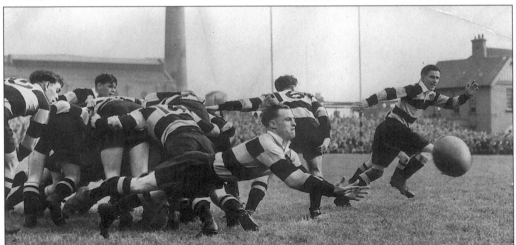

Newport's scrum-half, W.A. Williams, dive-passes at Rodney Parade while Cardiff's tail-gunner of a wing forward, C.D. Williams, gives chase of the ball and, no doubt, the waiting fly-half. Having carried the Olympic torch in 1948, 'CD' played for Cardiff against the Springboks and the All Blacks and then came out of retirement in 1957 to help defeat the Wallabies. Never one to do things in half measures he played on for another season as Cardiff captain in 1958/59.

A new name on Cardiff's fixture list in 1957 was that of Group Captain Ranji Walker's XV, who undertook a four-match autumn tour of South Wales. At the Arms Park they fielded a strong team with internationals such as Jeff Butterfield, Gordon Waddell and Phil Judd. They ran Cardiff close but the match-winning score came when Colin Howe went over for one of his career total of 14 tries.

A popular innovation in 1954 was the annual floodlit match with the Harlequins, played midweek at the White City Stadium in London. Not everyone approved of this departure from tradition – one match report noted that Cardiff played 'with the moon behind them in the first half' – but a big crowd turned up to see the 'Quins win 8-6 thanks to a late converted try. The following year they won again but in 1956, in front of a live television audience, Cardiff recorded their first win in the series when Cliff Morgan made a break, Gordon Wells scored the try and Alun Priday added the conversion. The floodlit matches continued until 1959, by which time Cardiff were also playing Bristol under lights.

Line-outs were a major feature of rugby in the 1950s and on average there would be at least twice as many as in the modern game. However, the crowds still turned out in great numbers. In this match against Newport, Colin Howe, at the front, assists the jumper, Roddie Evans, while at the very back (on the extreme left of the photograph) is Malcolm Gough, an excellent forward who played 224 games for the club.

The opponents change but the pattern of the game is similar. This match with Bristol in 1958 shows the South Upper Stand that had been completed the previous year. Cardiff are playing in their change strip of red jerseys.

Another development was the new Athletic Club premises that were opened in June 1956. The rugby was still played on the original Cardiff Arms Park, later to become the National Stadium (and now the Millennium Stadium site), and cricket was played on what is now the club ground. In the centre of this photograph is N.V.H. Riches, President of Cardiff Athletic Club. On his left is Charles Sergeant. Hubert Johnson (second right) is also present as is, on the extreme right, the rugby correspondent of the *Western Mail*, J.B.G. Thomas.

Hubert Johnson joined Cardiff Rugby Football Club in 1927, captained The Rags for three seasons in the 1930s and by the 1950s was in his prime as an administrator and committeeman. He was the public face of the club and, at the time of his death in June 1979, was president of Cardiff Athletic Club. Six months later the Hubert Johnson Room was opened in the clubhouse – an Aladdin's Cave of trophies, photographs and memorabilia 'Dedicated to rugby men throughout the world' and a permanent reminder of a supreme individual who was the spirit and lifeblood of the club throughout one of its greatest eras.

John Nelson, one of the club's greatest post-war forwards, in action against Llanelli at Stradey Park. He played in the 1953 team that beat New Zealand, came within a whisker of a Welsh cap in 1955, and two years later played for the Barbarians. He figured in six different positions in his 291 games for the first team but was primarily a blind-side wing-forward. Along with C.D. Williams and Sid Judd he formed a particularly effective back row. Shortly before his untimely death in January 2000, 'JD' Nelson was a popular nomination for the club's Hall of Fame.

After his playing days John Nelson became one of the club's most loyal and hard-working committee men. He was the honorary secretary, represented the rugby section on the management committee of the Athletic Club and was a founder member of the Former Players' Association.

Alun Priday was of the same generation as John Nelson and one of the most reliable full backs in club rugby for more than ten seasons. He won 2 caps for Wales, both against Ireland, in 1958 and 1961, but it was the Cardiff club that valued his true worth. He scored 100 points in a season seven times, when such a landmark was comparatively rare, and helped defeat the Wallabies in 1957. He also played against South Africa in 1960 and New Zealand in 1963 and retired after a serious injury at Bridgend in 1965 when his jaw was broken in a controversial incident. It was his 410th game for the first team and he finished with 1,799 points to his credit. After many years of outstanding committee work, including a period as secretary of the club, his election to the club's Hall of Fame in 1999 was richly deserved.

Players and committee men waiting happily alongside each other before the Penzance v. Cardiff match in 1958. Cardiff won the game itself, but the real victor was rugby and the spirit of camaraderie that was so prevalent throughout the 1950s.

Four

The Swinging Sixties

The 1960s really began with the visit of the South African touring team in 1960. They played three matches at Cardiff Arms Park, the second of which, against Wales on 3 December 1960, was played in torrential rain and a gale-force wind blowing from the Taff End of the ground. South Africa won the match by a solitary penalty goal. By the Sunday morning the entire ground was submerged in four feet of water as the Taff broke its banks. A great deal of damage was done to the Athletic Club as well, with many valuable club records being lost in the flood.

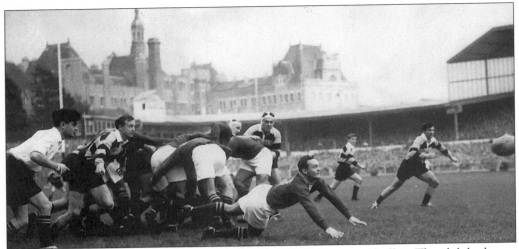

The Springboks match with Cardiff on 29 October 1960 was a torrid affair. The club had gone into the game unbeaten in thirteen matches that season and expectations were high but, watched by a crowd of over 50,000, any chance of a famous victory disappeared when open-side wing forward David Hayward was injured (but carried on) and fly-half Tommy McCarthy left the field before half-time with a broken collar bone. The Springboks won the match 13-nil. Here, their scrum-half Dick Lockyear dive-passes as Lloyd Williams comes around the scrum and Hayward sets off towards the opposition backs.

Lloyd Williams and David Hayward were two of the club's greatest servants from the mid-1950s until the mid-1960s. Both played more than 300 games in Blue and Black and both were captains for two seasons. Williams was a product of Cardiff Schools and Wales Youth and made his club debut at the age of nineteen in September 1952. However, he served a long apprenticeship under Rex Willis and Brian Mark before becoming a regular first choice scrum-half in 1956/57. He won the first of his 13 caps against Scotland in 1957, when Cliff Morgan was his half-back partner, and went on to lead Wales in his final three internationals. Hayward was one of the most constructive flankers of his generation. Originally from Crumlin, he joined Cardiff from Loughborough College in 1957 and played against the Wallabies, the Springboks and the All Blacks in the next six years. He won 6 caps for Wales in 1963 and 1964 and had played 325 first team games by the time of his retirement in 1967.

Alun Priday (right) with a fellow member of the club's Hall of Fame, Howard Norris. After making his club debut against Penarth in September 1958 at number eight, Norris went on to play in the second row and then become a prop forward good enough to win 2 caps for Wales and play in 3 tests for the British Lions in Australia and New Zealand in 1966. He played against four touring sides for the club, including the Springboks twice, and was also selected by the Barbarians to play against the 1967 All Blacks at Twickenham. In fourteen seasons he appeared 413 times for Cardiff and captained the club in 1967/68 and 1968/69 before devoting countless hours to committee work after his retirement.

Gordon Wells was a brilliant centre and wing and a gifted all-round athlete. Originally from Porth, he was educated at Cardiff University and St Luke's College, Exeter, and had already won the British triple-jump championship and played for Neath and Aberavon against the Springboks before he joined Cardiff, making his debut against Cardiff & District on 3 September 1952. He won his club cap in 1954/55 when he scored 17 tries in 34 games and he captained the club in 1959/60. By the time he retired in May 1962, Wells had scored 119 tries in 254 games. First capped by Wales in 1955, he won the last of his 7 caps in 1958. He was a great favourite with the Barbarians and toured Canada with them in 1957 and South Africa in 1958. After an outstanding display for Cardiff against the 1957 Wallabies, he was also selected for the Baa-Baas against them at the end of their tour. Gordon Wells died in April 1995, aged sixty-seven.

CARDIFF v. BRISTOL

AT NINIAN PARK
ASSOCIATION FOOTBALL GROUND
Kick off, 7-15 p.m.

Tuesday, March 14th, 1961

CARDIFF		BRISTOL	
1 A. J. PRIDAY	Full Back	J. M. LEWIS	A
2 R. GLASTONBURY	Right Wing	M. G. ELLERY	B
3 C. WILLIAMS	Right Centre	L. D. WATTS	C
4 M. ROBERTS	Left Centre	D. J. WEEKS	D
5 G. T. WELLS	Left Wing	J. RADFORD	E
6 B. DAVIES	Outside Half	J. M. BLAKE (Captain)	F
7 L. WILLIAMS (Captain)	Inside Half	B. W. REDWOOD	G
8 K. D. JONES	Forwards	D. St. G. HAZELL	H
9 W. J. THOMAS		A. N. OTHER	I
10 C. T. HOWE		R. V. GROVE	J
11 M. GOUGH		D. E. WATTS	K
12 W. G. DAVIES		D. J. MANN	L
13 D. J. HAYWARD		T. E. BASE	M
14 H. NORRIS		D. W. NEATE	N
15 E. WILLIAMS		L. DAVIES	O

Referee – – – Mr. R. McCOY (Cardiff)

THIS MATCH WAS ORIGINALLY SCHEDULED FOR NOVEMBER 3rd, 1960, BUT THE ATROCIOUS WEATHER AT THE TIME CAUSED POSTPONEMENT TO THE NEXT DATE, NOVEMBER 22nd.

ON THIS LATTER DATE THE WEATHER WAS AGAIN MOST UN-KIND AND A FURTHER POSTPONEMENT WAS NECESSARY.

IT IS HOPED THAT TONIGHT'S MATCH WILL BE PLAYED UNDER IDEAL CONDITIONS OF WEATHER AND LIGHTING AND THAT OUR SUPPORTERS WILL BE WELL COMPENSATED FOR THEIR TWO

Floodlit RUGBY Football

CARDIFF
v.
BRISTOL
at

Ninian Park A.F.C. Ground
on
Thursday, Nov. 3rd, 1960

Kick-off 7.15

Souvenir Programme · Price 6d.

RUGBY UNION FOOTBALL UNDER FLOODLIGHTS

THE INAUGURAL MATCH
FOR THE NEW FLOODLIGHTING SYSTEM

BRISTOL
v
CARDIFF

AT THE

MEMORIAL GROUND, FILTON AVENUE

ON

THURSDAY, OCTOBER 24TH, 1963

Kick Off 7.30 p.m.

———— : : ————

THERE WILL BE A SWITCHING-ON CEREMONY AT 7.25 p.m.

———— : : ————

P R O G R A M M E   3d.

The experiment of playing floodlit rugby that had started with games against Harlequins at the White City in 1954 was extended to two matches with Bristol at Ashton Gate in 1956 and 1957. They were again a huge success and when it was Cardiff's turn to be the hosts a game was arranged under floodlights at Ninian Park on 3 November 1960. Bad weather forced a three-week postponement to the event and then there was another delay on 22 November. At the third attempt the game was played, on 14 March 1961, Cardiff losing 14-19. Meirion Roberts (2), Gordon Wells and Glyn Williams scored Cardiff's tries with Alun Priday converting one of them. Much was made in the match programme about the hitherto unheard of innovation of Cardiff Rugby Football Club playing at Ninian Park, but the mood of the occasion was best illustrated by the soccer club's chairman, Ronald Beecher, when he wrote, 'For too long the rival codes have looked down at each other to the detriment of both, although our own relationship with officials and players of the Cardiff Rugby Club has been on the highest level for a number of years … On behalf of the Cardiff City Football Club, I extend the hand of friendship and welcome to our rugby friends.'

The Cardiff team that played the All Blacks in 1963 had a hard act to follow but were not expected to emulate their famous predecessors of ten years before. They had already lost six of their nineteen club fixtures in the lead-up to a match played in front of almost 50,000. Cardiff led 5-3 at half-time, thanks to a try by Cliff Howe (converted by Alun Priday) but a second-half dropped goal finally defeated a courageous club effort. On the evening before the game, President John F. Kennedy was assassinated and before the kick-off both teams and the spectators stood for a minute's silence. Cardiff's left wing was Richie Wills, an elegant player good enough to play in a Welsh trial. He later became an eminent artist whose portraits of Jack Matthews, Bleddyn Williams, Cliff Morgan and Rex Willis now hang in the Athletic Club. The man with the magic sponge was Tom Holley, one of the longest-serving helpers to be found in any rugby club. The Cardiff team group is, from left to right, back row: Haydn Wilkins (touch judge), Maurice Richards, Elwyn Williams, Graham Davies, Keith Rowlands, Cliff Howe, Richie Wills, Billy Thomas, Tom Holley (physiotherapist), D.M. Hughes (referee). Middle row: Lloyd Williams, Meirion Roberts, Howard Norris, David Hayward (captain), A.T. Thomas (chairman), Alun Priday, Kingsley Jones. Front row: Cliff Ashton, Steve Hughes.

Maurice Richards shot to fame when he scored four tries for Wales against England at Cardiff Arms Park. By this time he was already a British Lion, having toured South Africa in 1968 when he played in 3 tests. He had made his Cardiff debut in May 1963, playing for The Rags against Pontypool United at the age of eighteen years and two months and, five days later, for the first team against Glamorgan Wanderers. He soon became an automatic choice at either centre, where he played against the All Blacks in 1963, or wing, in a famed club three-quarter line in 1966/67 that had D. Ken Jones and Gerald Davies in the centre and Keri Jones and Richards on the wings. He scored 7 tries in his 9 games for Wales – all from on the wing – and by the time he transferred to Salford to play rugby league in October 1969 he had scored 97 tries in 171 games for Cardiff. In an equally distinguished career in the thirteen-a-side code, Maurice Richards scored 302 tries in 511 first-class matches, including 3 caps for Wales and 2 tests for Great Britain in Australia and New Zealand in 1974.

The four team groups of this double page are from the 1964/65 season and show the strength in depth at the club. After a gap of forty years, the Cardiff Extras XV was reintroduced to run alongside the first team and The Rags whilst the Youth continued to be a nursery that produced the senior players of the future. The first team captain was Meirion Roberts, an international centre blessed with an excellent pass, a direct style and a watertight defence. He played 8 times for Wales between 1960 and 1963 and was a member of the Barbarians XV that took the Springboks' unbeaten record at Cardiff Arms Park in 1961. From left to right, back row: A.D.S. Bowes, T.L. Williams, G.L. Porter, W. Lewis, P.T. Goodfellow, H. Johnson, A.T. Thomas, D.A. Brown, G. Davies, B. Mark. Middle row: L.B. Jones, W.H. Wilkins, Gary Davies, Tony Pender, John O'Shea, Elwyn Williams, Graham Davies, John Price, Alan Drew, Billy Thomas, C.T. Howe, W.R. Willis, T. Holley. Front row: David Hayward, Maurice Richards, Steve Hughes, R.F. Trott (honorary secretary), Meirion Roberts (captain), L.M. Spence (chairman), Howard Norris, Tom McCarthy, Billy Hullin, Tony Williams.

The Athletic XV were led by full-back Alan Drew. Apart from scoring 115 points himself he had the satisfaction of seeing his team lose only 5 times in 38 games – a reflection on a strong outfit that could call on great club men of the past, present and future, such as Ian Robinson, Lyn Baxter, John Davies and Frank Wilson. In this group are, from left to right, back row: T.L. Williams, G.L. Porter, W. Lewis, P.T. Goodfellow, H. Johnson, A.T. Thomas, D.A. Brown, C.T. Howe, B. Mark. Middle row: L.B. Jones, W.H. Wilkins, A.D.S. Bowes, A. Morgan, E. Morgan, J. Hickey, L. Baxter, I. Robinson, H.C. Ridgwell, G. Thomas, T.B. Williams, G. Davies, W.R. Willis, K. Ashton. Front row: J. Every, C. Jones, R. Duggan, R.F. Trott (Hon. Secretary), A. Drew (captain), L.M. Spence (chairman), J.H. Williams, J. Evans, F. Wilson, P. Thomas.

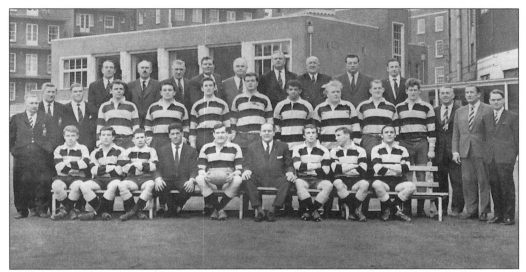

George Davey was at the helm of the Extras and they won 20 of their 26 matches in a season when seventy-six players were tried out, proving that this new team was an excellent testing ground for fresh faces. From left to right, back row: T.L. Williams, G.L. Porter, W. Lewis, P.T. Goodfellow, H. Johnson, D.A. Brown, A.T. Thomas, C.T. Howe, B. Mark. Middle row: L.B. Jones, W.H. Wilkins, A.D.S. Bowes, P. Tyler, G. Hughes, D. Hughes, R.J. Hearn, F. Wilson, A. Morgan, G. Thomas, G. Jones, G. Davies, W.R. Willis, K. Harse. Front row: J. Every, T. Sheppard, N. McJennett, R.F. Trott (Hon. Secretary), G. Davey (captain), L.M. Spence (chairman), R. Furness, J. Evans, A. Canham.

To complete this successful quartet, the Youth team also gained several honours under the captaincy of fly-half David Ivens. They lost only 5 games of the 26 played and won two sevens tournaments. From left to right, back row: T.L. Williams, G.L. Porter, W. Lewis, P.T. Goodfellow, H. Johnson, D.A. Brown, A.T. Thomas, G. Davies, B. Mark. Middle row: L.B. Jones, W.H. Wilkins, A.D.S. Bowes, G. Powell, D. Taylor, W. Breaden, A. Gulliford, T. Smith, J.J. Williams, R. Geddes, A. Williams, J. Southam, B. Davies, C.T. Howe, W.R. Willis. Front row: R. Taylor, G. Evans, P. John, R.F. Trott (Hon. Secretary), D. Ivens (captain), L.M. Spence (chairman), N. Williams, J. McCarthy, T. Stephenson, B.Rees.

The annual visit of the Barbarians on Easter Saturday continued to be the highlight of the season throughout the 1960s. The touring side were guaranteed to field a strong team, as witnessed by their 1964 line up that included household names such as Tom Kiernan, Mike Gibson, Mike Weston, Jim Telfer and Mike Campbell-Lamerton. Nevertheless, in that particular game Cardiff put on an outstanding display with prop Howard Norris scoring one of his team's four tries in a 21-3 win – Cardiff's highest score against the Baa-Baas since 1925. Later in 1964, on 7 October, the Barbarians returned to the Arms Park to play a special match to inaugurate the new floodlights that had been installed at a cost of nearly £6,000 – and on this occasion won the game 12-8.

Cardiff's other great traditional holiday match was against the Watsonians from Edinburgh at Christmas time. After a one-off game in 1896 they had visited Cardiff every year since 1927. Part of the tradition was that the touch-judges wore kilts and in this photograph of the 1965 fixture Colin Howe is clearly taking his duties very seriously. Cardiff often played in red jerseys against the Scottish side and here the Cardiff wing running alongside Howe is the legendary P. Lyn Jones.

The club's unbeaten record against Australia continued with another defeat of the Wallabies in 1966. This time the winning captain was Keith Rowlands, a six feet and five inch giant of a lock forward who had played for the Lions against the Springboks in 1962 and was later to become a rugby administrator at world level. His team for the game against the Wallabies contained several gifted players and a thrilling back division. The man-of-the-match was generally accepted to be scrum-half Billy Hullin, who scored a try and dropped a clever goal from right under the crossbar at the Taff End of the Arms Park. Two months later he won his Welsh cap against Scotland at Murrayfield. Cardiff won by 14-8, with D. Ken Jones also scoring a try and full back Ray Cheney adding a conversion and a penalty goal. From left to right, back row: Ron Lewis (referee), Phil Morgan, Tom Holley (physiotherapist), Maurice Richards, John Hickey, Lyn Baxter, Tony Pender, John O'Shea, Clive Evans, O.P. Bevan and K. Morgans (touch judges). Middle row: D. Ken Jones, Billy Hullin, Keith Rowlands (captain), Howard Norris, Billy Thomas. Front row: Keri Jones, Ray Cheney, Gerald Davies.

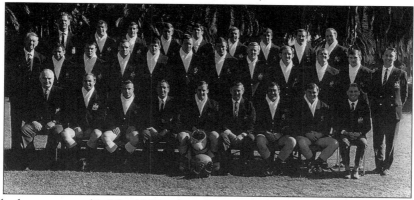

The club broke new ground in May 1967 with its first tour to the southern hemisphere. Five matches were played in South Africa and though the results may not at first glance appear to be have been exceptional – 2 wins, 2 defeats and a draw in 5 matches – the quality of the play was remarkable, especially in the 34-9 win over Eastern Province. With the nineteen-year-old Gareth Edwards at full back and inspired by what South African commentators described as 'the classical centre play of Gerald Davies and D. Ken Jones', Maurice Richards scored 3 tries on the left wing and added goal-kicking to his armoury to finish with 19 points. Jones had been the golden boy of the British Lions in South Africa in 1962. A wonderful mercurial talent with a deadly side-step and blinding pace, he first played for Wales and the Lions before his twenty-first birthday and when he arrived at Cardiff in the autumn of 1965, after a season out of the national team, he revitalised both his own play and that of the club. He went on a second Lions tour, to Australia and New Zealand, in 1966 and after his retirement from the game pursued a professional career in industry and business.

The demolition of the wooden North Stand that had been a feature of Cardiff Arms Park since 1934 began in the summer of 1968. Within two years club rugby would be played on the old cricket pitch in the shadow of the Westgate Street flats and a new National Stadium would be reserved for international and representative matches and Cardiff's games with major touring teams. By early 1969 the first signs of a new structure were evident.

Cardiff's first game at the new National Stadium, on the site of the old Arms Park, was on 13 December 1969, against South Africa. The new North Stand, backing onto the club ground, was not quite complete but a crowd of 28,000 saw the Springboks win 17-3. A mainstay of the club pack was John Hickey, seen here (centre) pulling back an opposing forward. He was one of the best uncapped back row forwards of his generation but Wales' loss was Cardiff's gain as he played 218 games in eleven seasons.

Five

To the Centenary and Beyond

King John and Prince Edwards ... although they had played together for Cardiff in the 1960s, the half-back partnership of Barry John and Gareth Edwards became world-famous during the early 1970s and will be remembered long before people recall that it was also the decade of the club's Centenary. With the pairing of these two heroes, Wales had won the Triple Crown and Five Nations Championship in 1969. They went on to share the title in 1970, and in 1971 and 1972 were unbeaten champions in seven Home Nations internationals (Wales did not travel to Dublin in 1972 because of violence in Ulster). John and Edwards also played key roles for the Lions in South Africa in 1968 and then, triumphantly, under Welsh coach Carwyn James and captain John Dawes in New Zealand in 1971; the following year Barry announced his early retirement.

The new club pitch at Cardiff Arms Park was in fact first used on 10 September 1969 when Cardiff Athletic beat Bristol United 14-3, although it was not to be officially opened for another thirteen months. That fact was no obstacle to a celebratory drink to toast the new pitch. From left to right are: Gwyn Porter (who had played 147 times for Cardiff either side of the war and then served twenty-five years on the committee), Alun Priday, Frank Trott (whose career had also spanned the wars while making 205 appearances at full back and then becoming secretary of the Athletic Club), Hubert Johnson (see page 48), John Davies (who was captaining The Rags in the match), Brian Mark (scrum-half with some 100 matches under his belt and a committee man since 1961), Mike Lawrence (Bristol United), A.T. Thomas and Haydn Wilkins (who first joined the committee in 1953 and who has held just about every position at the Arms Park).

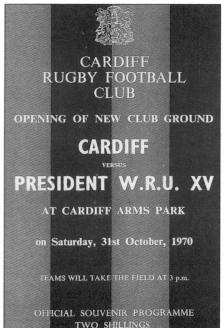

The programme cover for the official opening of the new club ground on 31 October 1970 when the Welsh President's XV, captained by Tom Kiernan of Ireland, included seven British Lions. Appropriately, the national president was Kenneth Harris, who had played such a positive and influential role in the negotiations between the WRU and the club, in the shape of Hubert Johnson, for the redevelopment of the Cardiff Arms Park complex.

Before the kick-off of the match with the President's XV *(above)*, made by the city's Lord Mayor, T.E. Merrels, seventeen former captains of the club paraded on the pitch . They were, *(below)* from left to right, standing: Jack Matthews (1945/46, 1946/47 and 1951/52), Bleddyn Williams (1953/54), Bill Tamplin (1950/51), Rex Willis (1952/53), Malcolm Collins (1955/56), Peter Goodfellow (1956/57), Eddie Thomas (1957/58), Lloyd Williams (1960/61 and 1961/2), David Hayward (1962/63 and 1963/64), Meirion Roberts (1964/65), Keith Rowlands (1965/66 and 1966/67), Howard Norris (1967/68 and 1968/69), John O'Shea (1969/70). Seated: Wilf Wooller (1938/39 and 1939/40), Les Spence (1936/37), Tommy Stone (1935/36), Tom Lewis (1932/33), Danny Davies (1925/26).

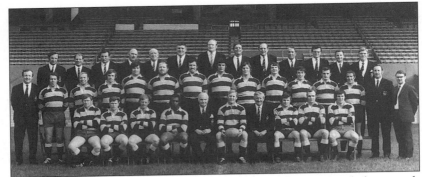

The Cardiff Athletic team in 1970/71 was a typical example of experienced players and promising youngsters. The committeemen in the back row for the most part appear elsewhere in the book. From left to right: David Hayward, Roy Bish, Colin Howe, Glyn Porter, Alun Thomas, Malcolm Collins, Keith Rowlands, Peter Goodfellow, Les Spence, T.L. Williams, Peter Nyhan (who in many years on the committee kept the club records and edited the programme), Brian Mark (another programme editor), Stan Bowes. Middle row: Lloyd Williams, John Uzzell, Tony Williams, J. Powell, W. Atwill, Maurice Braithwaite, Lyn Baxter, Phil Kallonas, Roger Lane, E. Williams, David Hoyle, J. Regan, Gary Samuel, Alun Priday, Keith Harse. Front row: Stuart Watkins, B. Neck, T. Stephenson, Carl Smith, Hubert Johnson, John Davies, Haydn Wilkins, Peter (RAF) Thomas, J. Hickey, Gary Davies. Bobby Windsor, who was to become one of the notorious Pontypool front row, made 5 appearances that season for The Rags and 4 for the Cardiff first XV. Among these characters, lock Maurice Braithwaite, yet another Cardiff player with a golden tenor voice, was an Englishman who cut his rugby teeth in Weston-Super-Mare and Pontypridd, and who was warned that he would never be selected for England if he played his rugby in Wales. A Welsh trialist on residential grounds, he captained a Welsh Universities XV, which included John Dawes, and went on to make nearly 100 appearances for Cardiff, while Stuart Watkins, 26 times capped by Wales, and John Uzzell had both joined from Newport.

This is not to say that the first club side of the decade lacked personality. The team that assembled for this group photograph in 1970 was, from left to right, back row: Dennis Gethin (later to become secretary of the WRU), Gary Davies, Gerry Wallace, Ian Robinson, Martin Truran, Tony Pender (a Cambridge blue and back-row forward who appeared 151 times), Mervyn John. Middle row: Gerald Davies, John Hickey, John O'Shea (captain), Gareth Edwards, Roy Duggan, John Bevan. Front row: Brian Coles, Ian Lewis. Hickey, an aggressive back-row man, came as a junior from Llandaff North and Canton to Cardiff Youth and was to captain the club in 1970/71. He played more than 220 times before staying on to lead The Rags. His brother, Dennis, had played 44 times in the 1960s and his father had played one game – against the Barbarians, curiously – in 1921.

As the captain of Cardiff during the centenary season of 1976/77, Gerald Davies was inevitably associated with many of the club's activities during the decade. But there was, of course, much more to it than that captaincy: he went on to lead the side for the next two years, thus becoming the first player since Gwyn Nicholls at the turn of the last century to serve three consecutive years as captain. Gerald, like Edwards and John a member of the Lions in South Africa in 1968 and in New Zealand in 1971, played 46 times at centre or wing for his country and, in 167 appearances for Cardiff, scored 68 tries, including a memorable four-timer at Pontypool in a cup-tie in 1979. Gerald, who had earned degrees at both Loughborough and Cambridge (whom he captained in 1970) and played with distinction for London Welsh, once scored five tries against Cardiff for Cambridge University on 17 October 1970.

The rugged free-scoring wing P.L. Lyn Jones – 'He'd go through 'em if he couldn't go round 'em,' said one colleague – goes over despite the close attentions of two Blackheath players in 1975. Jones may never have been capped by Wales, but his strike-rate while wearing blue and black was truly astonishing. In 1964/65, he scored 27 tries in 21 matches for Cardiff Youth, 10 for The Rags the following season and a further 28, including six against Old Penarthians, in 21 appearances the year after that. In 1967/68, he scored 15 times for the first XV and 16 for The Rags. Lyn was then leading try scorer for the Firsts in three consecutive seasons from 1969/70, top scorer with The Rags again in 1972/73 and continued to score for the First XV for several seasons thereafter. In all, he scored 120 tries in 226 first-team appearances and 119 tries in 100 matches for The Rags. P.L. Jones' son, Gareth, capped out of Bridgend, was also to play briefly for Cardiff during the 1990s.

Before he went north, John Bevan played only 35 times for Cardiff between 1969 and 1973 – but these were explosive years in which the former schoolboy international from the Rhondda made an enormous impact both through his 11 caps for Wales and for the successful British Lions in New Zealand in 1971. Later, in the 1990s, he became a part of the Welsh national coaching organisation. Bevan scored 25 tries in his short stay with Cardiff.

Gareth Edwards had a magnificent career for club, country and British Lions. When he left the international scene in 1978, he had a record number of caps for a scrum-half, having accumulated 53 (a feat which was later bettered by Robert Jones). The incomparable Gareth joined Cardiff in 1966/67 as a nineteen-year-old from Gwaen-cae-Gurwen, via Millfield College and Cardiff Training College (now UWIC), and by the time he was twenty-one, was captain of Wales and touring with the British Lions in South Africa. He helped his country to Grand Slams in 1970/71, 1975/76 and 1977/78, as well as to three other Triple Crowns, and was also a Lion on the famous New Zealand tour in 1971 and with Willie-John McBride's victorious team to South Africa in 1974. He is pictured here scoring for Cardiff (above) against the Overseas International XV in the centenary year celebration match which Cardiff won 24-15 and in Barbarian guise (below), as he torments the Australian defence with a typically deft touch. In twelve seasons for Cardiff, Edwards scored 67 tries in 195 appearances. He is now a non-executive director of the club.

What more can be said about Barry John? Basic statistics show that he played 93 times for Cardiff – as well as in many successful sevens matches – between 1967 and 1972, but that does not hint at the pleasure given to countless thousands by his elusiveness. 'It was always reassuring,' said one opponent ruefully, 'to see Barry go through a door and not through the wall'. This maestro's elegance, creativity, immaculate kicking out of hand and instant reading of a tactical situation were invaluable.

John's mastery was not confined to the Cardiff club, for whom he scored 24 tries and 30 dropped goals, including four in one match against his former club Llanelli on 28 October 1970, or even to the national side, by whom he was awarded 25 caps. Barry was also a key player in the Lions tour to South Africa in 1968 and to New Zealand in 1971, after which he announced his somewhat premature retirement at the age of twenty-seven.

As the years have gone by, his fame has not diminished. Among many other accolades, he was chosen as one of the first fifteen inductees to the International Hall of Fame in 1997. Included alongside him were fellow Cardiff legends Cliff Morgan and Gareth Edwards.

Cardiff broke new ground in the early 1970s when they visited Rhodesia despite some public protests because of Rhodesia's unilateral declaration of independence. The touring squad was, from left to right, back row: David Hayward, Gary Samuel, P.L. Jones, Mike Knill, Neil Williams, Bernard Hurley, Wayne Lewis, John Regan. Middle row: K. James (liaison), Gethin Edwards (brother of Gareth), John Davies, Roger Lane, Ian Robinson, Lyn Baxter, Phil Kallonas, Roger Beard, Mervyn John, John Harding, Tom Holley (trainer and rub-a-dub man for more than twenty-five years). Front row: Hubert Johnson, Gareth Edwards, Alex Finlayson, Colin Howe (chairman), John James, Malcolm Collins, Tony Williams, Garry Davies, Haydn Wilkins (secretary). Skipper Gerry Wallace was missing on safari when this picture was taken. Cardiff won all six matches, including the encounter with the Rhodesian national team, who were beaten 24-6.

Many names could appear on a list of Cardiff's best and/or unluckiest uncapped players and for those who watched the club during the 1960s and '70s the case of flanker Mervyn John was particularly poignant. Mervyn, who made his debut in 1967/68, went on to make 319 appearances and captained the club in their pre-centenary season of 1974/75, scoring 86 tries – including one in all five matches of the Rhodesian tour – and appearing in final Welsh trials. He also served many years on the committee, managed the club on overseas tours and was a member of the board of Cardiff RFC plc when the game became professional and the club a limited company.

As always with a Cardiff party, there was plenty of singing in Rhodesia. Here, it's Gary Samuel who conducts the heavenly chorus during a tour that took in visits to the Victoria Falls, game reserves and the Kariba Dam.

Once back from Rhodesia, Cardiff faced rather more difficult opposition in November 1972 when they met the New Zealanders. Despite the efforts of Gareth Edwards, pictured here kicking to safety, Cardiff were unable to repeat epic earlier victories and went down 20-4.

On 1 November 1975, the touring Australians met Cardiff for the fifth time – and lost for the fifth time. Here, Brynmor Williams, one of a plethora of fine scrum-halves on the Cardiff books, sets another attack moving during the 14-9 win. By this time the centenary year was approaching.

James Callaghan, then Prime Minister and MP for Cardiff South East (second right), is welcomed to the Cardiff Centenary Banquet by the club chairman, Les Spence (see *Images of Sport: Cardiff Rugby Football Club 1876-1939*), Ewan Davies (who had played for Cardiff between 1909 and 1912 and was, in 1975, at the age of eighty-nine the oldest living Welsh international) and Gerald Davies, the club captain. The event was held in a marquee in the Castle Grounds.

Above: The Cardiff team during centenary season, 1976/77. From left to right, back row: Chris Padfield (coach), John Evans, J. Kelleher (referee), C.G.P. Thomas (touch judge), Alan Phillips, Bob Dudley-Jones, Roger Lane, Ian Robinson, Carl Smith, Mike Knill, Trevor Worgan, John Davies, Meirion Joseph (touch judge), J.E. Davies. Middle row: Tom Holley, Mike Murphy, Paul Evans, Gareth Edwards, Alun Priday (secretary), Gerald Davies (captain), Les Spence (chairman), Barry Nelmes, Chris Camilleri, Alex Finlayson, Tony Williams. Front row: Terry Holmes, Stuart Lane, Mark McJennett, Mike Watkins, Gerry Wallace, Peter Bolland (who was to be a 'breakaway' referee during the rebel season of the 1989/90). *Below*: The complete staff of the club in that 100th year of its existence.

To celebrate the end of the centenary season, it was a happy – and rather smart – party that left for Canada for an unbeaten six-match tour.

Wing and centre Alex Finlayson, a policeman who won 3 caps for Wales, played first for Cardiff in 1967/68, when he scored 13 tries for The Rags. He led the First XV scoring the following season with 18 and, later, he scored 20 tries in 1972/73, topping the list once more in 1973/74 with 31 and again in 1974/75 with 15.

Although the huge crowds of the immediate post-war years were not to be repeated, there were matches that still drew in the masses – even in the snow, as this cup-tie at Pontypool Park on 10 February 1979 demonstrates. Here, Pontypool's Peter Lewis avoids Stuart Lane only to be confronted by Cardiff captain Barry Nelmes. In fact, the match was abandoned after only 27 minutes, Cardiff eventually winning 23-12 when the game was replayed a fortnight later. Cup-ties at Pontypool invariably provided excitement: the previous year, Gerald Davies had scored four times in a 16-11 win – he touched the ball only three times in the second half but ran in three match-winning tries.

Barry Nelmes was twice vice-captain under Gerald Davies and was himself made captain for 1978/79. Nelmes, a prop who joined Cardiff from Bristol in 1973/74 and went on to make 166 appearances for the club, became the first player to be chosen for England while playing for Cardiff in 1976.

Roger Beard, caricatured (*top left*) by Derek
Stears, who illustrated the Quidnunc column in
the Cardiff programme for many years, was a
rumbustuous, no-nonsense prop who played 164
times for Cardiff and was to be an influential
coach behind cup-winning sides in the 1980s.
Known affectionately during that period as 'Mr
Nasty', he was also a famed expert at the
traditional rugby clubhouse drinking game of
Cardinal Puff. *Top right:* Carl Smith, a versatile
forward who made 238 appearances for the
club, was sadly unable to go on the tour to
South Africa because of that country's policy at
the time of apartheid – but he was widely
respected on the Welsh scene. Lyn Baxter (*left*)
was a highly-rated lock forward and yet another
Cardiff player unlucky not to be capped. He
had already been on a Welsh tour to Argentina
(when caps were not awarded) when, on
1 January 1971 during a final Welsh trial in
which he was having a splendid match, he
dislocated an elbow while scoring a try.
Another chance never came. Despite an
altercation with the club at one stage in his
career, Lyn made 290 appearances.

Left: Ian Robinson in line-out battle with the notorious Swansea lock Geoff Wheel. 'Robbo' was said to be the tallest man to represent Wales so far when he won the first of his 2 caps in 1974 as an uncompromising forward. He made 384 appearances for Cardiff and later served for many years on the committee. The brothers Roger (*below left*) and Stuart Lane (*below right*) gave remarkable service to Cardiff during the 1970s and '80s. Roger joined in 1970/71, earned a final Welsh trial and, at one stage, shared the club's try-scoring record for a forward with 16 in 1972/73. The versatile Stuart, who joined that season, won 5 caps for Wales and was chosen for a disastrous (for him) British Lions tour; after less than two minutes of rugby, he was injured and had to return home from South Africa.

Cardiff supporters have followed the club round the world and continue to do so today with the European involvement in the Heineken Cup. Here, they also sample Welsh history as, during a club tour to South Africa, they drop in at Rorke's Drift, where so many Welshmen won medals during the Zulu wars.

The flourishing Cardiff Rugby Supporters Club has for many years held award nights. Ted John, the popular long-term chairman, is seen with three recipients in the 1970s: Gareth Davies, Terry Holmes and Stuart Lane.

Back in South Africa, it's a scrum-halves' get-together as Lloyd Williams, Brian Mark, Brynmor Williams and Terry Holmes meet up with the famous South African administrator and former player Danie Craven, whose influence in world rugby was huge.

It was an action-packed tour. Cardiff are pictured here on the move in Pretoria.

The club's centenary year, 1975/76, had seen Cardiff receive a trophy from royalty (*above left*) when the Prince of Wales presented the Snelling Cup, the major sevens competition of the day, to Chris Camilleri, a dashing wing three-quarter and talented sevens performer. Watching the proceedings are two men who had enormous influence in the club, Hubert Johnson, President of Cardiff Athletic Club (after whom the Trophy Room is named), and Les Spence, a stalwart player before the war who was to be a long-term committee man and club chairman during Centenary Year and later to become President of the Welsh Rugby Union and of the Athletic Club. Camilleri's talents were not restricted to the sevens: during his career he scored 73 tries in 125 appearances, including one against Llanelli (*above*) when J.J. Williams was rendered helpless. Prince Charles was again present (*left*) when, in 1994, he saw jubilant captain Mike Hall lift the Swalec Cup after beating Llanelli 15-8. But this is to get ahead of ourselves, for this was by no means the first time that Cardiff had won the major Welsh knock-out tournament ... there was the little matter of a famous spell during the 1980s.

Six
The Cup Runneth Over

Cardiff won the Schweppes Cup five times during the 1980s – and in three of the victories they were led by the charismatic English number eight John Scott. 'Scotty', a Devonian who played for his county at the age of seventeen and who was the youngest-ever forward to have an English trial, initially impressed everyone while at Rosslyn Park and then came to Wales to improve his game. He had a formidable understanding with scrum-half Terry Holmes and captained Cardiff for four seasons from 1980 to 1984 as well as skippering his national side in South Africa while winning 35 caps for his country.

Outside-half Gareth Davies and John Scott (above) played major roles in the successes of Cardiff during the 1980s – although the date on the Arms Park billboard behind them may be misleading as it was still celebrating the Cardiff centenary several years earlier. Gareth Davies (pictured again below) was to participate in just about every aspect of club life as player, captain and, eventually, when the club became a plc, as its first chief executive. In 361 matches for Cardiff, he became the club's record scorer with 3,117 points, made up of 77 tries, 458 penalties, 623 conversions and 63 drop goals. In addition, he was capped 21 times by Wales and was a British Lion in South Africa in 1980. Davies, Scott and the front row of Eidman, Phillips and Whitefoot were to play in all five Cardiff cup-winning sides of the decade.

Bob Lakin, a Vale of Glamorgan farmer who was to be one of the longer-serving Cardiff stars never to play for Wales (despite a 'B' cap), plunges over from the tail of a line-out to score the opening try as Cardiff win the Schweppes Cup for the first time in 1980/81 by beating Bridgend 14-6. Bob had been made captain of The Rags for the season, but actually missed only four first team games. Later, he was to serve on the Cardiff committee and become a club director after having 324 first-team outings for the club.

The Cardiff side that beat Bridgend. From left to right, back row: Ken Rowlands (touch judge), Derrick Preece, Stuart Lane (reserve), Ian Eidman, Kevin Edwards, Bob Norster (reserve), Tony Mogridge, Bob Lakin, Terry Lee (reserve), Brian Lease, Ken Swaine (reserve), Clive Norling (touch judge), Alun Richards (referee). Middle row: Mike Watkins (reserve), Neil Hutchings (who scored the second Cardiff try), Steve Evans, Glyn Davies, John Scott (captain), Alan Phillips, Jeff Whitefoot, David Burcher, David Barry (reserve). Front row: Terry Holmes, Gareth Davies. Mike Watkins, the substitute Cardiff hooker, was to captain Newport against Cardiff in the final five years later.

Along with Ian Eidman, the Cardiff front row of Jeff Whitefoot (*centre*) and Alan Phillips (*left*) were to go on to be part of the team in the next four cup-winning years, as well as to represent Wales. Whitefoot was to be capped 19 times while making 305 Cardiff appearances and Phillips, who joined in 1973/74 when he won his Rags cap, was to go on to make a record-breaking 470 appearances for Cardiff, during which he also scored the most tries by a forward (162). A robust and uncompromising competitor, he won 18 caps for Wales, skippered his club and went on to become a part of the WRU coaching and team management hierarchy.

Bob Norster (see page 87) was another forward to go on to higher things after he had moved to Cardiff from Abertillery. Assisted by Bob Lakin, he prepares for line-out action against the formidable opposition of Pontypool's Eddie Butler and Jeff Squire.

Ian Eidman's first-ever try for Cardiff came in the 1981/82 final – he was ultimately to score only 4 times in 227 appearances – and was crucial. The 14-caps tight-head prop was on hand to support the dynamic charge *(above)* by Kevin Edwards, who had a formidable game, to score the only try *(below)* in a 12-12 draw. Schweppes Cup regulations at the time stated that the team scoring more tries in a draw would win the match. Not only did Cardiff retain the trophy, but they also won the unofficial *Western Mail* club championship for the first time in twenty-four years. Edwards was to play in four of the five successful Cardiff cup sides of the 1980s and made a total of 157 appearances in blue and black.

By the time of the next cup win in 1983/84, Bob Norster had arrived from Abertillery and here he savours beating Neath 24-10 in the final with, from left to right: Jeff Whitefoot, John Scott, Gareth Davies, Terry Holmes, Alun Donovan and Owen Golding. Wing Gerald Cordle scored one of the tries and flanker Golding the other, with Gareth Davies converting both and kicking four penalties. The outside-half for Neath that day was Jonathan Davies, who was to join Cardiff a decade later after taking rugby league by storm. Cordle was also to score in 1987 when Cardiff beat Swansea.

Owen Golding, who also scored in the final, plunges over for a try in the 26-6 semi-final win over Llanelli at St Helens, Swansea. Many felt that this would have made a more fitting final; in the event, it was Neath who very nearly provided the surprise by stretching Cardiff to the limit.

Robert Norster was one of the great Welsh lock forwards. He dominated the line-out for both club and country, thoroughly earning his British Lions places in New Zealand in 1983 and Australia in 1989. The holder of a Fine Arts degree, Bob was capped 34 times by Wales, appeared for his club on 252 occasions and, by the end of the Millennium season, was back at the Arms Park as Cardiff team manager.

Terry Holmes made his first senior appearance (helping to win at Newport) while captain of Cardiff Youth in the 1974/75 season, when Gareth Edwards and Brynmor Williams were still on the books. He was to go on to great things in both rugby union and league. Captain of both club and country, he won 25 caps and scored 142 tries in 216 Cardiff appearances, forming a formidable partnership with both his number eight John Scott and his out-half Gareth Davies.

Adrian Hadley, named man-of-the-match and thus winner of the coveted Lloyd Lewis Memorial Trophy, scores one of his three tries – the first hat-trick in a Schweppes Cup final – as Cardiff beat Newport 28-21 on 26 April 1986. Neil O'Brien, at scrum-half after Terry Holmes had gone north, also scored a try, which Gareth Davies converted in addition to kicking two penalties.

Terry Holmes, a superb successor at scrum-half to Gareth Edwards, sets his backs moving yet again here to cause problems for Aberavon. He was later to be a major part of the Cardiff coaching set-up under Alex Evans. On the right is Terry Charles, nephew of soccer legend John.

The Cardiff team that beat Swansea 16-15 to win the Schweppes Cup in 1986/87. From left to right, back row: Winston Jones (referee), Roger Beard (coach), Jeff Whitefoot, Ian Eidman, Mark Ring, Bob Lakin, Howard Stone, Gareth Roberts, Bob Norster, John Scott, Tim Crothers, Richard Cardus, Clive Norling (touch judge), Derek Bevan (touch judge), Ron Ayres (physiotherapist). Front row: Steve 'Wally' Blackmore, Neil O'Brien, Gerry Cordle, Mike Rayer, Chris Hutchings, Alun Donovan, Alan Phillips (captain), Geraint John, Adrian Hadley, David Evans, Ian Greenslade.

Howard Stone, who played second row for Cardiff alongside Bob Norster against Swansea, has been one of Cardiff's most loyal servants, playing 291 times for the senior side. As Youth, Rags and Senior XV lock and back-row man, Howard excelled, but thought that he had reached the height of his career with a Wales 'B' cap against France in 1988. To his surprise, in 1993 at the age of thirty-one, 'The Fox', as he was known, was playing so well that he won a Wales 'A' cap and a place on the bench with the Welsh side against Ireland. To cap it all, in 2000 he coached the Cardiff team to victory over Llanelli in the Welsh Youth Rugby Union Cup final.

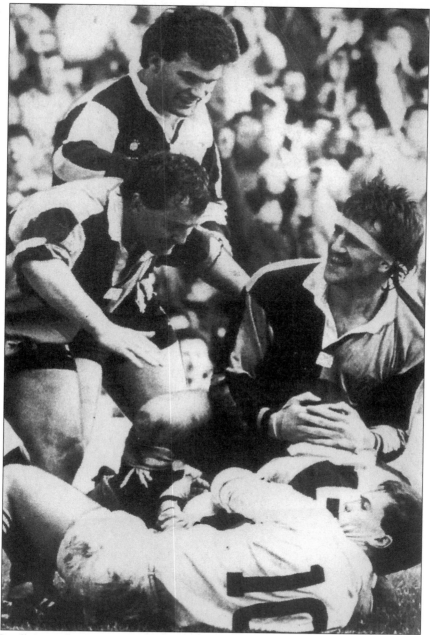

Gerald Cordle's try during Cardiff's 1986/87 Schweppes Cup final win over Swansea is greeted with a congratulatory hug from Bob Norster while skipper Alan Phillips and Tim Crothers, who came on as a replacement for Gareth Roberts, also relish the moment. Just as Gary Pearce had done to thwart Cardiff's hopes and win the cup for Llanelli in 1984/85, so Mike Rayer dropped a goal for Cardiff to win this 1986/87 final. Four of the Swansea team that day – David Young, who was to captain the Arms Park team in 1998/1999 and play for Cardiff both before and after starring in rugby league, Malcolm Dacey, Arthur Emyr and Robert Jones – were later to wear blue and black jerseys.

Cardiff maintained their 100 per cent record against the Wallabies with a 16-12 win in 1984. Here, Adrian Hadley receives Alun Donovan's pass on his way to a try. Hadley, who was to join Rugby League in 1988, played 27 times for Wales.

Gareth 'Ming' Roberts, who joined from Swansea and made a big contribution to the back row in the cup years (and also won 7 Welsh caps), has in support another former Swansea colleague, Alun Donovan. Centre Alun, known as 'Lonnie' through the similarity of name with a 1950s skiffle group leader, played in two of the successful cup sides after also gaining a cup medal with Swansea. He won 5 caps and became part of the Cardiff coaching set-up for several years.

The summer of 1988 found Cardiff on a prestigious short and successful trip to New Zealand, during which they won two of the three matches. The touring party was, from left to right, back row: John Hadley, Gareth Roberts, Justin Burnell, Mark Rowley, Matthew Parry, Tim Crothers, Jeff Whitefoot. Middle row: Ian Greenslade, Owen Golding, Steve Crandon, Chris Conway, Andrew Martin, Mr H.K. Gower (of the sponsors Rizla), Chris Collins, Ray Giles, Malcolm Dacey, Chris Hutchings, Mike Rayer. Front row: Gerald Cordle, Ron Ayres (physiotherapist), Alan Phillips, Mervyn John (manager), Alun Donovan (captain), Tony Williams (assistant manager), Howard Stone, Roger Beard (coach), Steve Blackmore.

The following year, 1989, the New Zealanders were back in Cardiff and, although number eight Mark Edwards was able to cross for this try, Cardiff were beaten 25-15, despite being 9-3 in front at the interval.

Unpredictably effervescent, Mark Ring, who came up through the club's Youth, was one of the more colourful and charismatic Cardiff and Wales personalities through the 1980s and early '90s. Capped by his country 32 times, the precocious playmaker scored 94 tries in 262 appearances for the club, either at out-half or in the centre. Even after returning from a serious leg injury, he rarely belied his reputation as a crowd-pleaser. Not all of Ringo's activities met with official approval, however – on one occasion against London Welsh he attempted a conversion with a back-heel.

Sadly, as the 1980s drew to a close, so was the year approaching when the Barbarians would no longer be annual visitors. Full houses were almost guaranteed at the Arms Park to watch star-studded teams. *Above*: In 1986, from John Scott on the left, via Terry Holmes with the ball, to Swansea and England's Keith Colclough on the right, you can pick out the names. *Below*: In this action from 1989, Bob Norster sets a Cardiff attack on the move watched by Tim Crothers, Howard Stone, Jeff Whitefoot and Steve Blackmore (yet another prop who was to be capped from the club and serve on the committee).

There were others who contributed to those splendid Cardiff sides of the 1980s which, arguably, saw the last of the truly amateur days as professionalism was just around the corner. There were few to match, for example, the Corinthian spirit of Pat Daniels (*left*) who, on one occasion, was having a quiet drink in his Llandaff local on Friday evening when a phone call from the WRU hierarchy in the Angel Hotel demanded his immediate presence as a replacement for an international the following day. Pat returned to his friends for another pint before obeying. Pat, a centre and wing who started life with Glamorgan Wanderers and who won 2 Welsh caps and toured Australia with the national side, is nailed here by Terry Cobner of the Barbarians. Rhodri Lewis (*right*) had won 5 Welsh caps in the early 1980s and had a fine track record with Cardiff.

There was, in short, no lack of personalities in the Cardiff sides. Richard Cardus (*left*), for example, was an English international who had won a cup medal with Wasps the year before playing for Cardiff in their 1986/87 final victory over Swansea. A colleague in that team, Tim Crothers, who was Cardiff through and through, became, in 1989/90, the fifth Old Cantonian to skipper the club following R.A. Cornish, Les Spence, Peter Goodfellow and C.D. Williams. But times were changing.

Seven

Leagues, Professionalism and the New Era

Cardiff won the Heineken League championship for the first time in 1994/95. League rugby had been introduced in Wales in September 1990 and, despite two runners-up positions in the first four seasons, the club was felt to be seriously under-achieving. An ignominious ninth place in 1991/92 brought matters to a head and, under the captaincy of Mike Hall and the coaching of Alex Evans, the club won 18 of its 22 league matches to take the title in April 1995.

The road to the 1995 championship had begun three years before with the appointment of the Australian Alex Evans – 'Call me Alec' – as coach and the beginning of Mike Hall's three-year tenure as club captain. The club chairman was Mervyn John (left of Mike Hall in the photograph) and the assistant coach to Evans was the highly-respected Terry Holmes (on the extreme right). At the end of the 1992/93 season the chairman was to write: 'Before the domestic season commenced, we had already laid our trump card – Robert Alexander Cheyne Evans from Queensland, Australia – a man with a proven record of achievement as an international rugby coach, with a pedigree and without any preconceived ideas of Cardiff RFC and its personnel … In my twenty-five years with Cardiff I have never before experienced a start where the spirit was so strong and the players were visibly bubbling with confidence and anticipation.' The team lost only 8 of its 37 games in all competitions and it was a period when some of the greatest names of the 1990s came to the fore. By the end of the season, Mike Budd, Adrian Davies, Jonathan Humphreys, Colin Laity, Kevin Matthews, Hemi Taylor and Nigel Walker had won their club

caps and Davies had scored 290 points. The former Olympic hurdler Walker had arrived on the Welsh rugby scene like a meteor, scoring 21 tries in 20 games and winning his Welsh cap within six months. On 9 January 1993, Plymouth Albion were beaten by a club record 107-3, with Ceri Thomas scoring 37 points. From left to right, back row: Malcolm Childs, Ian Eidman, Peter Goodfellow, Terry Charles, Ian Robinson, Chris Webber, Robert Lakin. Fourth row: Alun Donovan, John Evans, Brian Mark, Andrew Lewis, Mike Rayer, Kevin Matthews, Adrian Davies, Simon Hill, Tony Williams, Gary Davies, Jim O'Donnell, Steve Cannon. Third row: Alex Evans, Gwynne Griffiths, Brian Bennett, Nigel Walker, Ceri Thomas, Andy Moore, Colin Laity, Tony Rees, Owain Williams, Jason Allen, Paul Armstrong, Huw Bevan, Keith Davies, Ron Ayres, Bob Newman, Terry Holmes. Second row: Stuart Roy, Paul Kawulok, Steve Ford, Mike Budd, Mervyn John (chairman), Mike Hall (captain), John Nelson (secretary), Hemi Taylor, Jonathan Humphreys, Howard Stone, Derwyn Jones, Mike Griffiths. Front row: Geraint Lewis, Jason Hewlett, Andy Booth, Adam Palfrey, Chris John, Chris Mills.

Mike Hall was one of the most successful captains of the club in modern times. Under his leadership, Cardiff won the Swalec Cup in 1994 and the Heineken League twelve months later. A strong, direct centre with a water-tight defence, he made his club debut on 13 January 1990 at Aberavon and after three consecutive seasons as club captain he led the side again in his 193rd and final first team game at West Hartlepool on 4 April 1999. He also scored 77 tries for the club. Originally from Bridgend, Hall won Cambridge blues as a student and gained his first cap as a replacement in New Zealand in 1988. A year later he toured Australia with the British Lions and played in the first test. He also captained Wales in the 1995 World Cup in South Africa before retiring from international rugby with 42 caps to his name.

When Cardiff won the Swalec Cup for the first time in seven years in 1994 (*opposite, above*), the decisive try was scored by Mike Rayer. In front of a crowd of 52,000 at the National Stadium, the full-back gave a masterly display as a last-line of defence – and he could attack with deadly effect. His try against Llanelli just before half-time took the score to 15-8 and there were no further scores in the second half. Rayer made his club debut on 10 April 1985 and won cup-winners' medals in 1986 and 1987 – when he dropped the winning goal in extra-time against Swansea. Apart from a two-year spell with Bedford, 'Mikey' Rayer was an ever present in the Cardiff side for fifteen years and by the start of the 2000/01 season he was approaching 350 first team games, 100 tries and 1,500 points. He was cruelly under-used by Wales at the peak of his career, but still won 21 caps and played for the Barbarians against Australia at Twickenham. When The Rags were re-established as the Under-21 development squad in September 2000, Rayer was a popular choice to assist with the coaching.

The Cardiff teams of the mid-1990s were strong in all areas, but the fifteen-man rugby was only possible because of the solid platform provided by the pack. Not all the players were superstars. The nucleus was an ever-reliable group of solid club forwards. Huw Bevan, at the back of this line-out, was a hooker good enough to play for Wales at schoolboy and student levels and pushed Jonathan Humphreys all the way for first-team selection. After injury forced him to retire, he became a much-respected fitness coach before moving to take up a similar post in Bridgend in 1999. Tony Rees is in the centre of the photograph. Rees was the archetypal front-of-the-line jumper and the perfect foil to Derwyn Jones as a lock partner. He was a member of the 1994 cup-winning team and also played for Wales 'B' and for the French club Brive when they won the Heineken Cup. And at the front of the line is Andrew Lewis, a modern prop in 25 games for Wales, who was then earmarked as a hooker and began a second international career in that role in the autumn of 2000.

Left: The advent of professional rugby in September 1995 suddenly opened up the prospect of leading players who had gone north to play rugby league returning to Wales to play union again. From day one of this new era attention was focused on Jonathan Davies, the charismatic fly-half who had left Llanelli nearly seven years before to become equally successful playing for Widnes, Warrington and Great Britain. With the help of the Jewson Group, club officials brokered a deal that brought Jonathan Davies back to South Wales. Amidst huge media interest and in front of a live television audience he made his Cardiff debut – at full back – against Aberavon on Sunday 5 November 1995. *Right:* Adrian Davies came from the classical school of Welsh fly-half play. A reliable goal kicker who scored a record 264 points in the Welsh League in 1992/93, he possessed the vital knack of biding his time before making the midfield break that invariably took opposition defences by surprise. His half-back partnership with Andy Moore spearheaded the club's drive for honours and made the pair great favourites, both as individuals and as a unit, with the club's supporters. Adrian Davies played four times for Cambridge in the University Match at Twickenham – he also gained a soccer blue – and won 9 caps for Wales, including the 1995 World Cup.

A crucial factor in the success of the team in the 1990s was the sense of togetherness on and off the field. The squad that developed between 1992 and 1995 had a great belief in the methods and proven track record of coach Alex Evans; if they put in a sub-standard performance, they expected to face the music. Here, though, the boot is on the other foot, Evans being serenaded by four vital members of his successful side: Jonathan Humphreys, Derwyn Jones, Hemi Taylor and Adrian Davies.

Steve Ford, watched by team-mates Jonathan Davies and Owain Williams, races away for his fifth try in the cup match against Dinas Powys on 22 February 1997. The touchdown was his 187th in 217 games for the club, passing the record try tally of 185 by Bleddyn Williams (which had stood since 1955). Ford had made his club debut on 10 April 1985 and also won 8 caps for Wales. By the time he finished his Cardiff career in 1998 and returned to his local club, Rumney, Steve Ford had extended his total number of tries for Cardiff to 198, including 76 in 99 games in the league.

Steve Ford's record try haul was a cause for celebration and one of the first to congratulate him was Bleddyn Williams. After Ford and Williams in the all-time list for club try scorers come Gerald Cordle (164), Alan Phillips (162), John L. Williams (150) and Arthur Cornish (149).

Cardiff *v*. Swansea in 1989 and the opposing scrum-halves are Andy Moore and the All Whites' Robert Jones. Moore was a product of Cardiff Youth, educated at Llanishen High School and winner of an Oxford blue. After several years of unstinting service for the club he was selected for the Wales' World Cup campaign in 1995 and eventually played 4 times for Wales. Jones, by contrast, was capped as a twenty-year-old in 1986 and went on to become the most-capped Welsh scrum-half of all time with 54 appearances. He played one season for Cardiff in 1998/99. Ironically during that season, when Cardiff withdrew from the Welsh League and played the English clubs, Andy Moore captained Richmond against the blue and blacks at the Madejski Stadium and his opposite number was Robert Jones. Two months later Moore returned to the Arms Park to make a guest appearance for the club against Bedford.

The final game played at the National Stadium, Cardiff Arms Park before its demolition and redevelopment as the Millennium Stadium was the Swalec Cup final between Cardiff and Swansea on 26 April 1997. Cardiff won the match by 33-26. The great memory of an historic day was a try by Nigel Walker early in the second half when he raced sixty metres along the north touchline past four defenders, the last of whom, Stuart Davies, is seen being left helpless as Walker glides around on an arc to the goal posts at the Westgate Street end of the stadium. It was a piece of individual brilliance fit for the occasion and, despite coming under great Swansea pressure in the dying moments, Cardiff held on to lift the cup for the seventh time.

At the end of a triumphant lap of honour a tired but happy Cardiff squad show off the cup and their individual tankards. Cardiff's try scorers in the final were Justin Thomas, Mike Hall and Nigel Walker, whilst Lee Jarvis kicked 18 points with four penalty goals and three conversions. Centre Leigh Davies was voted man of the match. In this photograph, replacement Jonathan Davies has already commandeered a Swansea shirt while alongside him at the back are Derwyn Jones, Keith Stewart, Lee Jarvis (with the cup), Owain Williams, Lyndon Mustoe, John Wakeford, Simon Hill and Paul Young. At the front are Justin Thomas, Jason Hewlett, Mike Hall, Jonathan Humphreys and Robert Howley.

In opposition here but soon to become team-mates are two great back row forwards, Emyr Lewis and, in the colours of Rugby Canada, Dan Baugh. Lewis joined Cardiff from Llanelli in 1994 and was a number eight forward of the highest class. By the time he suffered a serious back injury on the Wales tour of Australia in 1996 he had become the most-capped back row forward for Wales with 41 appearances. His injury was career-threatening but he showed great courage in recovering to become a key member of the championship-winning side of 1999/2000, a season in which he also played his 100th game for the club and was recalled to the national squad. Dan Baugh had come to the attention of the club playing in the ill-fated Challenge Trophy matches of 1998 when overseas teams took on the top Welsh clubs and Cardiff reached the final against Pontypridd. After playing briefly as a replacement against Bath in February 1998 – he was known as 'D. Brown' in the interests of anonymity! – Baugh signed a two-year contract with the club in September of that year and that was happily extended in September 2000, by which time his deadly tackling and dynamic play had made him an automatic choice for his country and a major personality with the club's fans.

In September 1998 Cardiff and Swansea embarked on a season of friendly fixtures with the top English sides. The two clubs, worried about falling attendances and a lack of competitive matches in the domestic league, had campaigned with several other Welsh and English clubs for an official British League to start that season. When negotiations broke down in August, a full list of Anglo-Welsh matches for Cardiff and Swansea were announced. Reaction within the club and particularly from the supporters was positive, with several hundred travelling to Bedford for the first match on 5 September 1998. Cardiff won the game by 27-10 with the honour of the first try to be scored going to Jonathan Humphreys early in the second half.

A week later, the first of the home matches against English opposition attracted a crowd of 10,021 to the Arms Park. The opponents were Saracens, captained by the British Lion Tony Diprose and including test players from South Africa, Argentina, Australia, France, Ireland and England in their ranks. Cardiff won the game by 40-19 and set off on a series of home matches that were to attract large crowds at home and several coach loads of supporters for away matches. In this photograph, Liam Botham, who had joined the club in October 1997 and who was to score 24 tries in 29 matches during 1998/99, tackles Saracens' fly-half Alain Penaud. The following season Botham was called into the England squad and joined Newcastle Falcons in the summer of 2000.

Gareth Thomas was typical of the new breed of attacking three-quarter that were the stars of the professional rugby age. At six feet three inches tall and weighing sixteen and a half stones, he was bigger than most international forwards of barely twenty years before. But he was also faster: in his first 50 games he scored 36 tries at wing or centre. He was equally successful at international level with a hat-trick on his debut in the 1995 World Cup and four tries against Italy in 1999. Thomas, originally from Bridgend, joined Cardiff in December 1997 and by the start of the 2000/01 season only Ieuan Evans, Gerald Davies and Scott Gibbs had won more caps as a three-quarter for Wales.

If the backs were getting bigger then the forwards were also getting taller. On 5 March 1993, the club invited Derwyn Jones to play in a friendly game against Bective Rangers and shortly after that in the Easter Saturday match against the Barbarians. Barely eighteen months later he was winning the first of his 19 caps for Wales against South Africa. Jones hailed from Pontarddulais and had played for Neath and Llanelli and studied at Loughborough College. At six feet ten inches, Jones was the tallest man to play for Wales and was a key element in the success of the Cardiff team in league, cup and European competitions until he left the club in May 1999 to play a season for Beziers in France. After that he retired from first-class rugby at the age of twenty-nine to begin a new career as a teacher and broadcaster.

The advent of professional rugby union in September 1995 precipitated many changes in the administration of the game at club and national level. Cardiff Rugby Football Club was amongst the first to respond to these needs and on 15 May 1996 the new company of Cardiff Rugby Football Club plc was incorporated. It was re-registered as a private company limited by shares on 16 December 1996 and on 1 February 1997 it acquired the business and net liabilities of the rugby section of Cardiff Athletic Club. During this first period of the company's existence, the directors appointed were Peter Thomas, as chairman, Gareth Davies, as chief executive, Bleddyn Rees and Simon Webber. Dr C.D. Williams also served as a director between November 1996 and April 1997. On 10 June 1997, further appointments to the board of directors were Paul Bailey, Gareth Edwards, Alex Evans, Patrick Gore, Mervyn John, Alan Peterson and John R. Smart. This early photograph of the directors, taken in the Hubert Johnson Room, is a timely reminder that, whatever the changing face of modern rugby, the heritage of the club remains very important to these men. From left to right, back row: Simon Webber, Alan Peterson, Mervyn John, Gareth Edwards, Gareth Davies. Front row: Bleddyn Rees, Peter Thomas, John R. Smart.

Eight

Into Europe

Club rugby entered a new era in 1995 with the introduction of the Heineken Cup. For the first time the major clubs would compete in an official European competition that would attract a wider public and provide an even higher standard of rugby for the top players. Nothing summed up the attraction of the Heineken Cup better than the quarter-final tie between Cardiff and Bath on 16 November 1996 in front of a capacity crowd at Cardiff Arms Park. Cardiff won the match 22-19. The turning point was a try in the second half by Nigel Walker as he finished off a move started by Hemi Taylor and taken on by Robert Howley, Jonathan Davies and Mike Hall.

Cardiff had established their European credentials from the very beginning, qualifying from their pool matches in 1995 to play in a semi-final at Lansdowne Road, Dublin. The game was played on 30 December in icy, wet conditions that had prevented a plane load of supporters leaving South Wales. Leinster were Ireland's inter-provincial champions but were well-beaten by an outstanding team effort by Cardiff. Captain Hemi Taylor scored the first try by the posts following a magnificent charge by Emyr Lewis. Taylor was another key member of the side in the 1990s. Having arrived at the same time as Alex Evans in 1992, his direct approach at number eight perfectly suited the team's style of play. Although he was originally from Morrinsville in New Zealand, he had lived in Wales since 1986 and was soon attracting the interest of the Welsh selectors. He eventually won the first of his 24 caps in 1994 and captained the club for two seasons before joining the coaching staff in 1998.

Cardiff's second try in the semi-final was scored by Mike Hall after one of his favourite moves, touching down in the corner after a decoy run from a scrum by Andy Moore. The scrum-half added a drop goal of his own in the second half to complete a famous 23-14 victory that took Cardiff into the first-ever final of the Heineken Cup.

The first Heineken Cup final was played on Sunday 7 January 1996 at the National Stadium, Cardiff, in front of more than 22,000 spectators and a live national television audience. Cardiff's opponents were the French champions Toulouse, who had beaten Swansea 30-3 in their semi-final. They threatened to do the same to Cardiff with two spectacular tries in the opening ten minutes, but the blue and blacks stayed in the game with five penalty goals by Adrian Davies, the last of these from nearly 50 metres forcing an extra time period of thirty minutes. Here, Jonathan Davies competes for the ball with Thomas Castaignede.

Nigel Walker fails to break away. Cardiff were unable to penetrate Toulouse's defence and although each side added another penalty goal to take the score to 18-18, a cruel penalty decision in front of Cardiff's posts in the dying moments of extra time gave the French side victory and the inaugural Heineken Cup with a narrow 21-18 victory.

Two great former players assisted Alex Evans on the coaching staff in 1992 and took over when Evans returned to Australia in December 1995. The esteem in which Terry Holmes was held as a player stood him in good stead for his new role as head coach. He had blue and black blood running through his veins and soon proved his credentials as a successful club coach. In the first month he guided Cardiff to the Heineken Cup final, to be followed by victory in the Swalec Cup final in April 1997. With him was Tony Faulkner, known affectionately at 'Charlie', a legendary prop from the Pontypool stable of the 1970s. He was one third of a much-feared front row and had won 19 caps for Wales, the last of these coming at the age of thirty-eight, and had been on a Lions tour to New Zealand. He was the ideal man to take charge of the new breed of Cardiff front row forwards, including Lyndon Mustoe, Andrew Lewis, Phil Sedgemore and Jonathan Humphreys.

Alex Evans left Cardiff at the end of 1995 to take up an appointment as director of rugby with the Australian Rugby Union. Earlier in the year he had been coach of Wales for the World Cup in South Africa, combining that with his club duties. Two years later, he returned briefly for a second spell but finally returned to his homeland in 1998 to be part of the successful coaching team that led Australia to victory in the 1999 World Cup.

Good sides know how to celebrate – as Lee Jarvis and Robert Howley clearly demonstrate. In this photograph, Cardiff have just beaten Harlequins 32-31 at The Stoop in Twickenham in a vital Heineken Pool game in 1997. Defeat would have meant almost certain elimination from the competition but by winning this game, and another the following week at home to Bourgoin, the club maintained its record of never having failed to qualify for the knock-out stages in Europe and did so again in 2001. Against Harlequins, Howley had scored the first of Cardiff's four tries as early as the fourth minute. Jarvis had gone one better, however, dropping a goal a mere 27 seconds after the start of the game. He was an exceptional goalkicker who eventually scored 1,167 points in 88 games for Cardiff before returning to his native Pontypridd in 1999.

One of the great moments in Cardiff's Heineken Cup history – Jonathan Davies won the game at Wasps with an opportunist dropped goal as the final whistle was about to blow. The London side had just taken the lead themselves with the score at 24-23 but, from Cardiff's restart, Emyr Lewis regained possession and back went the ball from Robert Howley to the fly-half. The kick flew over from 40 metres and Cardiff had won 26-24. A year earlier, Jonathan Davies had appealed for supporters and well-wishers to be patient as he readjusted to the fifteen-a-side game and his opportunities had been limited for the rest of that season. But now, twelve months later, he was spearheading Cardiff's challenge in the Heineken Cup and playing for Wales at half-back with club partner Robert Howley against Australia. He finally retired at the end of the 1996/97 season.

A new face in the Cardiff team at the start of the 1997/98 season was Gregori Kacala. He arrived from French club Brive, having been a member of their Heineken Cup-winning team earlier in the year – they had beaten Leicester in the final at the National Stadium. Originally he was from Poland and had won 27 caps for his country as they rose through the ranks of Eastern European rugby. At six feet four inches tall and more than seventeen stones in weight, Kacala soon established himself as one of the best ball carriers in the game. He was also incredibly durable. Despite regular injuries he played on through the pain barrier and in his first two seasons at the club he played in 60 games, mainly at number eight.

Another overseas player who became a great favourite with the Cardiff faithful was lock forward John Tait. He also arrived in the autumn of 1997 in the wake of glowing reports concerning his performance for Canada against Wales in Toronto that summer. As well as being an extremely dextrous ball-carrier, 'Taity', as he quickly became known, was a magnificent cover-tackler as his rangy six feet eight inch frame seemed to get to all parts of the pitch. He played 27 games in his first season and was voted Player of the Year by the Supporters' Club. He represented Canada in the World Cup and by the end of 2000 had won 30 caps for his country. He had also been joined at the club by his younger brother, Luke, another lock who completed his sixth form education in Cwmcarn and played for Wales Schools and then for Wales Youth in the Junior World Cup in France.

In a decade of many great club men and popular personalities, Jonathan Humphreys would be near the top of everyone's list as a player who represented all that was best about Cardiff Rugby Football Club. He played his first game as hooker on 1 September 1989 and passed the 200 landmark in October 2000. During those eleven years he had captained the club for one season and led the side on many other occasions. His indomitable spirit and courageous tackling – he was synonymous with the new jargon of 'big hits' – endeared him to thousands of fans. He was also a great disciple of the Alex Evans school of coaching from day one and under the Australian's guidance his career prospered. He won his first cap for Wales against New Zealand in the 1995 World Cup at Ellis Park, Johannesburg and three months later returned to South Africa as captain of his country. He was to lead Wales 17 times before handing over the reins to team-mate Gwyn Jones.

Another stalwart of the 1990s was Simon Hill. His early games were as a centre alongside Mark Ring, but by 1993 he was good enough as a wing to tour Zimbabwe and Namibia with Wales, playing in all six games and winning his first cap. He also toured with Wales in Australia in 1996 and went on to play in 12 internationals and complete ten seasons with Cardiff. During that time he won two league championships and also a Swalec Cup-winner's medal in 1997. A great club man in every sense, he lived in Llantwit Major and balanced his sporting aspirations with his professional career as a dentist. The club awarded Simon Hill a testimonial in January 2000 in recognition of his outstanding service, including 116 tries in 241 games.

Craig Morgan was one of the first of an exciting young generation of backs to emerge at the end of the 1990s. He was quickly selected by Wales Under-21 as a full-back and then by Wales 'A' in his best position, on the wing. His try-scoring feats were phenomenal and he reached his 50th try for the club in only his 58th game, while also hitting the headlines for scoring tries in 17 consecutive games.

The saddest story of modern Cardiff rugby is that of Gwyn Jones. He joined the club from Llanelli in 1996 and was appointed captain of Wales the following summer. A dynamic open-side flanker, he was considered one of the best in his position and missed selection for the British Lions to South Africa after a shoulder operation forced him to miss half a season of domestic rugby. Worse was to follow. On 13 December 1997, while playing for Cardiff against Swansea at the Arms Park, he was caught in a ruck with his head forced down on his chest, causing what his consultant neurosurgeon described as 'flexion and axle stress'. He was paralysed for several months and it was a cruel end to a potentially great rugby career. Mercifully, Gwyn Jones, through his own courage and determination as well as expert care and attention, made a good recovery. At the time of the accident he was on a two-year sabbatical from his medical studies, but as his strength grew in 1999 he established himself as an astute sportswriter and television commentator in both Welsh and English.

Cardiff's successes in Europe were sometimes built on disappointments. A typical example was the heavy defeat in a pool match in Montferrand in November 1999. The pacy French side scored six tries in a 46-13 defeat that threatened to derail the blue and blacks' bandwagon. Cardiff's solitary try was scored by open-side flanker Martyn Williams. He had joined the club from Pontypridd earlier in the year and was an international forward with enormous potential. He had already captained a Wales XV in a match against the USA and finished the season with 21 appearances out of a possible 23 and was chosen as the Player of the Season at the Champions' Dinner. Cardiff recovered from the pounding in France to win the return match at the Arms Park 30-5 and later qualify for the Heineken Cup quarter-finals.

A new coaching staff was appointed at the beginning of the 1999/2000 season. With Robert Norster as team manager, the head coach was Lynn Howells (*left*), assisted by Geraint John. Howells arrived with a proven track record of success at Pontypridd, where he had worked with Dennis John when that club had won league and cup honours. He was also Graham Henry's assistant with the national squad and successfully managed the fine balancing act between club and country as Cardiff won the Welsh/Scottish league in his first season in charge. *Right*: Geraint John was a former Cardiff player – in 171 games between 1980 and 1995 he scored 704 points at fly-half and centre – and was considered one of the brightest young coaches in Wales. After an earlier spell at Cardiff, as well as Llanelli, he returned to take charge of the backs and oversee the club's new development programme. This would lead to the re-establishment of the under-21s, known as The Rags, in September 2000.

Nine
The Millennium Experience

The first-ever Welsh/Scottish League was established in September 1999. It comprised ten Welsh clubs and the two Scottish super-districts, Glasgow Caledonians and Edinburgh Reivers. Cardiff's first eight matches were played while the Rugby World Cup was also taking place. As no fewer than thirteen of the club's players were involved in the latter, several players were drafted into the squad on short-term contracts. After a shaky start when they lost at Newport and Llanelli, they recovered to leave the team well-placed when the stars returned. Between 25 September 1999 and 10 May 2000, Cardiff won 17 consecutive league matches to win the title with three games to spare. Appropriately, vice-captain Mike Rayer, who had led the team during the World Cup, received the trophy amidst traditional celebrations.

A key factor in Cardiff's success was the signing of fly-half Neil Jenkins. After ten years with Pontypridd, during which he broke every conceivable points-scoring record, he brought stability and decision-making to Cardiff's midfield with a notable effect on players such as Gareth Thomas and Leigh Davies in the centre. He had become the highest points-scorer ever in international rugby during the World Cup and by February 2001 had passed the 1000 points mark in 81 games for Wales and 3 Tests for the Lions – and soon set about piling up the points in the blue and black jersey. In his debut game at Swansea, on 13 November 1999, he kicked 19 points in Cardiff's 34-25 win and followed that with 22 points against Harlequins in the Heineken Cup and 25 in Italy against Treviso. By the end of his first season his tally was 228 in 14 matches and he started the following season by passing the 200 points barrier again in only his eleventh game.

Robert Howley had been Neil Jenkins' half-back partner in 30 internationals by the end of 2000. He had first joined Cardiff briefly during the autumn of 1993, but returned to his home town of Bridgend after only 5 games. However, three years later he settled at the Arms Park to become the latest in a long line of great scrum-halves who have played for Cardiff, Wales and the British Lions. Howley's game was based on power and pace and he became a key member of the team that chased domestic and European titles. In the 1997 Swalec Cup semi-final, the second of his two tries in an outstanding victory over Llanelli covered 80 metres as he burst around the front of a defensive lineout and raced along the touchline. His Lions tour to South Africa that summer was cut short by a shoulder injury, but in 1998 he became captain of Wales in succession to Gwyn Jones. He led his country 22 times, which included ten straight victories and a World Cup campaign. Cardiff also benefited from these qualities of leadership as he stood in for David Young at the start of the 2000/01 season and led the team with distinction.

A feature of the modern Cardiff squad is the balance of youth and experience, home-grown talent and astute recruitment. Spencer John (*left*)was originally from Neath, started his senior rugby at Llanelli and was capped by Wales in 1995 aged twenty-one – unusually young for an international prop. He joined Cardiff in 1997, an excellent acquisition who could play both on the loose-head and tight-head sides of the scrum. He was a strong, effective ball-carrier who would play week in, week out. In the two seasons between September 1998 and May 2000, he played in 62 of the club's 69 matches and was deservedly recalled to the national squad. Jamie Robinson (*right*) was educated at Ysgol Gyfun Glantaf in the city and shot to prominence during 1999, playing for the Wales team that reached the final of the FIRA Junior World Cup. He made his first team debut against Sale on his nineteenth birthday. A year on, he was a star in the Wales Development Tour of Canada. A silky centre of the old school, with an innate sense of the well-timed pass to release his team mates, he seems destined for top honours in the twenty-first century.

Rhys Williams (*left*) was a contemporary of Robinson, though educated at Cowbridge Comprehensive. He was another star billing, for the 1999 Junior World Cup, and out-performed his friend by graduating to senior honours in twelve months. Originally a centre, he became a daring, counter-attacking full back of great pace – ideally suited to modern rugby. His senior debut for Wales came at Lansdowne Road, Dublin on 1 April 2000, when his sense of adventure surprised Ireland and contributed to an important 23-19 victory. Pieter Muller (*right*) arrived in Cardiff in the summer of 2000, aged thirty-one with 33 caps for South Africa. It proved an inspired signing by the management, as the ex-Springbok was the ideal foil at Neil Jenkins' elbow. Defences were sucked in, allowing Robinson, Williams and the outside backs to take full advantage of their pace. His play in the vital Heineken Cup match at Saracens, when Cardiff scored four tries with thrilling, attacking rugby, confirmed his arrival on the blue and black scene and won him a man-of-the-match award.

Another young player destined for a major role in Cardiff's continuing success is wing Nick Walne. He first played for the club against the Barbarians while on vacation from Cambridge University – where he won three blues – and joined on a permanent basis in May 1999. He had already played for Wales and went on to be a member of the World Cup squad. A tall, graceful wing in the classic tradition, his first season at the club will be remembered for his six tries in one match against Dunvant on 25 March 2000. Cardiff won the game – it was a league fixture – by a record 116-0. Walne's six tries was not a club record, however, as in 1878 Percy Heard had scored seven against Blaenavon at the Arms Park and at Christmas 1893 Dai Fitzgerald had run in six against London Welsh. The only comparable feat in modern times was when Derrick Preece (*below, left*) scored six tries in a Schweppes Cup tie at Gowerton on 18 December 1982. Cardiff's 116 points against Dunvant beat the previous aggregate of 107 against Plymouth Albion in January 1993 when Ceri Thomas (*below, right*) had a record personal points tally of 37.

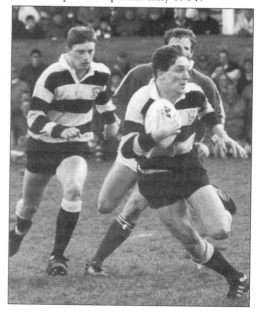

Every decade of Cardiff Rugby Club's proud history has been enriched by players who have brought, through their positive attitude and honest endeavour, further honours to the club as well as themselves. Amateur may have given way to professional, but the values remain essentially unchanged. No one epitomised the last decade of the twentieth century better than Owain Llewellyn Williams, a rangy back-row forward from Ogmore-by-Sea who joined the club in 1992. He immediately showed a readiness for hard work and, in the modern jargon, putting his body on the line, that endeared him to all the club's supporters. Other 'star' players came and sometimes went, but Owain was always available in any position in the back row. During the 1998/99 season he celebrated his thirty-fourth birthday but still played in 37 of the 38 matches; two years later he was captaining the Wales team in sevens tournaments as far afield as Heidelberg, Durban and Dubai. He had won his only cap for Wales in the full version of the game ten years before. The photograph goes some way towards demonstrating the affinity between Owain Williams and the Arms Park crowd. It was taken in May 2000 when he led out the team for his 200th game.

The Cardiff team of 2000 was in safe hands with the re-appointment, for the third consecutive season, of David Young as captain. A world class tight-head prop, he is a leader with the respect of all the players, coaches and back room staff around him. He first joined the club in 1988, having already won the first of his 44 caps for Wales as a nineteen-year-old against England in the previous year's World Cup. He was also part of the Triple Crown-winning team of 1988 and, now a blue and black, toured Australia with the Lions in 1989. He formed a Test-winning front row with England hooker Brian Moore and Scotland's David Sole. Young played rugby league between 1990 and 1996, when he captained Salford and Wales – leadership is second nature to him. As a youngster he captained Wales Schools and Wales Youth and in January 2000 he took over from his club colleague Robert Howley as captain of the senior side in the Six Nations championship. It was the natural progression and sat easily alongside his club stewardship, where his quiet but formidable presence had established him as one of the outstanding figures in the post-war history of the club. It was a sixty-year pageant of success and transformation that started under Dr Jack Matthews and ended with David Young – and with every likelihood of further progress in the years to come.

The twentieth century had ended appropriately with the establishment of the club's Hall of Fame. It was a near impossible task to identify the first fifteen names regardless of position to be the first inductees. Expediency dictated that they should be living legends who had played between 1945 and 1990 and who represented all that was best about Cardiff Rugby Football Club, both on and off the field. At a gala dinner on the eve of the 1999 World Cup the fifteen were announced as: Dr Jack Matthews, Bleddyn Williams, Rex Willis, John Nelson, Cliff Morgan, Alun Priday, Lloyd Williams, Howard Norris, Gerald Davies, Gareth Edwards, Barry John, Gareth Davies, Terry Holmes, Alan Phillips and Robert Norster. Cliff Morgan, who was unable to attend the first dinner, was eventually presented with his award by fellow all-time great Jack Matthews on the occasion of the Champions Dinner the following summer.

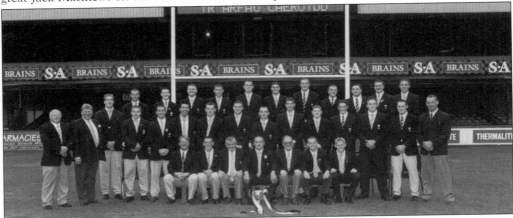

A final indication that the future good health of the club was in safe hands came in the spring of 2000 when Cardiff Youth won the Welsh Rugby Union Cup for a record eighth time at the Millennium Stadium. They beat Llanelli Youth 18-6 with tries scored by Owain Ashman and Karl Rees, with Chris Anderson converting one and adding two penalty goals. The Cardiff squad and officials are pictured with the trophy at Cardiff Arms Park. Cardiff had previously won the competition in 1980, 1981, 1984, 1985, 1991, 1992 and 1995 and were runners-up in 1983, 1986 and 1998. From left to right, back row: Dean Watkins, Chris Miller, Geraint Kettley, Owain Ashman, James Goodall, Matthew Hodge, Andrew Gardner, Khalid Jama, John Stringer, Daniel Evans, Lee Mullane. Middle row: Colin Davies, Bill Woods, Luke Tait, Alun Davidson, Rob Lamb, Geraint Cook, Gareth Rowley, Joe Barnes, Scott Headington, James Turner, Chris Reddicliffe, Nick McLeod, Nathan Llewellyn, Phil John, Howard Stone. Front row: Gerry Roberts, Nick Wakley, Mr J.D. O'Donnell (chairman), Greg Woods (captain), Mike Ryan, Karl Rees, Chris Anderson.